Sensory Integration and Self-Regulation in Infants and Toddlers:
Helping Very Young Children Interact With Their Environment

Sensory Integration and Self-Regulation in Infants and Toddlers:

Helping Very Young Children Interact With Their Environment

G. GORDON WILLIAMSON, PhD, OTR

MARIE E. ANZALONE, ScD, OTR

ZERO
TO
THREE®

Washington, DC

**Sensory Integration and
Self-Regulation in Infants and Toddlers:**
Helping Very Young Children Interact With Their Environment

Authors: G. Gordon Williamson, PhD, OTR
Marie E. Anzalone, ScD., OTR

Series Editor: Emily Fenichel

Designer: Susan Lehmann, Washington, DC
Photo credits: Barbara Young, cover, pp. 36, 56
Marilyn Nolt, p. 57

Published by:
ZERO TO THREE: National Center for Infants, Toddlers and Families
Phone: (202) 638-1144
Toll-free phone number for orders: (800) 899-4301
Fax: (202) 638-0851
Web: www.zerotothree.org

ISBN: 0-943657-06-7
Printed in the United States of America

Acknowledgment

ZERO TO THREE gratefully acknowledges the generous support of the A.L. Mailman Family Foundation, which has nurtured so many pioneering efforts in the infant/family field and has made this publication possible.

This volume is the first in a planned new series of "research to practice" publications from **ZERO TO THREE**: National Center for Infants, Toddlers and Families. Each volume will provide an overview of an area of research of importance to the growing infant/family field and discuss its implications for direct practice with infants, toddlers and families.

ZERO TO THREE is a national nonprofit organization whose mission is to promote the healthy development of our nation's infants and toddlers by supporting and strengthening families, communities, and those who work on their behalf. We are dedicated to advancing current knowledge; promoting beneficial policies and practices; communicating research and best practices to a wide variety of audiences; and providing training, technical assistance, and leadership development.

For more information about these issues and the resources available from ZERO TO THREE, please visit our Web site at:
www.zerotothree.org

Executive Director: Matthew E. Melmed

Contents

Acknowlegment v

Preface ix

CHAPTER ONE
Sensory Systems and Sensory Integration 1

Seven sensory modalities 5

The tactile system 6
The vestibular system 7
The proprioceptive system 9

Attributes of sensory stimuli 10

The process of sensory integration 12

Components of the sensory integrative process 13

Summary 15

CHAPTER TWO
Observing Sensory-Based Behavior in Infants and Young Children in Context 17

The "four A's" of infancy 18

Sensory-related behavior in the context of the environment: Goodness-of-fit 22

The story of Madeline 23

Summary 25

CHAPTER THREE
Patterns of Sensory Integration 27

Sensory modulation and sensory threshold 28

Sensory modulation profiles 32

Praxis and dyspraxia 36

Diagnostic classification of sensory-related mental health and developmental disorders of infants and toddlers 40

Regulatory Disorders 40

Multisystem Developmental Disorder 43
Summary 46

CHAPTER FOUR
Assessment 47

General guidelines for screening and assessment of sensory integration 48

Qualitative observation 52
Observation of the child 52
Observation of the context 56

Parent interview and questionnaires 58
The sensory diet 59
Standardized questionnaires 60

Standardized instruments 62

Interpreting assessment data 65

Summary 69

CHAPTER FIVE
Intervention 71

Collaborative work with parents 71

Modifying the environment to grade children's sensory experience 75

Direct intervention 85

Intervention guidelines 94
Intervention for children with hyperreactivity 95
Intervention for children with hyporeactivity 102
Intervention for children with dyspraxia 105

Summary 110

APPENDIX A
Play in the Context of Sensory-Based Intervention 111

APPENDIX B
Strategies To Enhance Self-initiation and Adaptive Behavior 117

References 123

Authors 129

Preface

Every child has a unique pattern of taking in and responding to information from the senses about their world and their bodies—an individual profile of sensory preferences and tolerances. Every child must also cope with a unique environment, composed of all the adults and children, places and things, sights, sounds, smells, textures, flavors, routines, transitions, and interruptions that make up daily life.

Most very young children become increasingly adept at taking in what they see, hear, and feel and organizing this sensory information in a purposeful way to regulate their own behavior. Children do this so naturally and independently that parents are often amazed at the changes that can occur in a single month as their child begins, for example, to sleep through the night, giggle at funny noises, or comfort herself when upset. Some children explore their world and master its challenges with ease and zest. Many other children learn to build on their own capacities and accept help from others as they delight in success and manage the frustration intrinsic to new learning. Still other children require a great deal of assistance in order to overcome difficulties in sensory processing and achieve the levels of self-regulation needed to successfully interact with and explore their environment.

Because so many people have important roles to play in helping infants and young children interact with their environment, we have written this monograph for a broad, multidisciplinary audience of service providers, researchers, and policy makers serving young children and their families. The monograph is targeted to a wide array of disciplines from the medical, therapeutic, educational, mental health, and psychosocial fields. It is appropriate for practitioners who work in a variety of settings—child care, early intervention, neonatal intensive care follow-up, developmental clinics, infant mental health centers, child life programs, social service agencies, and preschools. Some parents and family members may also find the content useful. This monograph is designed to help readers:

1. understand the sensory development of infants and young children;

2. learn about assessment and intervention approaches designed to promote very young children's self-regulation and adaptive behavior; and

3. become aware of new directions and outstanding questions in basic and applied research in this field.

As authors, we come to this work with several decades of training and research in occupational therapy, special education, and early intervention. Perhaps more important, we bring a keen interest in trying to integrate and synthesize current thinking about the sensory and motor development of infants and young children in the fields of occupational therapy, neuroscience, child development, psychology, psychiatry, education, and the movement sciences. Five major strands of inquiry have been particularly important to us:

1. sensory integration, as developed and practiced by Jean Ayres (1972, 1985) and modified by others;

2. principles of occupational therapy, particularly those discussed by Wendy Coster (1998), Simmie Cynkin (1990), and Janice Burke (1998);

3. investigations into the self-regulatory behavior of infants, especially the work of Heidelise Als (1986; 1982), T. Berry Brazelton (1992; 1990; 1984), and Claire Kopp (1982);

4. concepts in infant mental health, notably those described by Stanley Greenspan (1992), Daniel Stern (1985), and Serena Wieder (Greenspan & Wieder, 1997; Lieberman, Wieder, & Fenichel, 1997); and

5. research on temperament and infant perception by Stella Chess (1977), Eleanor Gibson (1988), Jerome Kagan (1997), and Mary Rothbart (1981), among others.

This monograph focuses on children from birth to three years of age, but its perspectives and principles are relevant for work with all young children. We discuss the sensory integration and self-regulation of children across the developmental continuum, from infants and toddlers who are developing typically to those with severe difficulties. When children are developmentally "on target," recognizing their unique patterns of sensory preferences and tolerances helps parents and caregivers interact with them more effectively. When development is not progressing as expected, sensory integration deficits may underlie difficulties. Problems in sensory integration may occur in young children with a variety of diagnostic conditions, including prematurity, prenatal drug exposure, colicky-baby syndrome, learning disabilities, autism spectrum disorders, language delay, cerebral palsy, spina bifida, and Down syndrome. Acquired sensory deficits are also seen in children with a history of abuse, neglect, and traumatic stress disorder. Although these are very different diagnoses, difficulties in sensory processing may occur in each of them.

As practitioners, we are committed to understanding individual differences in the sensory development of young children so that we can support parents in their role as caregivers, promote a goodness-of-fit between the child and the environment, and intervene to directly remediate children's underlying sensory processing deficits. In this monograph, we describe practical approaches to assessment, diagnosis, and intervention that are designed to understand and enhance young children's sensory processing. These approaches focus on:

1. capturing individual differences in self-regulation of behavior;

2. an individualized, problem-solving approach to intervention planning;

3. attention to intervention strategies which become an integral part of the child's everyday activities and routines; and, finally,

4. introduction of more specialized intervention strategies that require additional training.

To guide the reader on this journey, we have ordered our discussion as follows:

Chapter 1, Sensory Systems and Sensory Integration, describes the modalities through which we receive sensory input from our external surroundings and our bodies and introduces the concept of sensory integration, which involves organizing sensation for adaptive use.

Chapter 2, Observing Sensory-Based Behavior in Infants and Young Children in Context, provides a framework for understanding how the sensory integrative process is revealed in the behavior of infants and young children, particularly with respect to the "four A's" of infancy—arousal, attention, affect, and action.

Chapter 3, Patterns of Sensory Integration, introduces the concepts of sensory modulation and praxis, which allow us to describe sensory-based behavioral patterns of young children. This chapter introduces several frameworks for classifying problems in sensory integration and self-regulation.

Chapter 4, Assessment, presents guidelines and methods for the screening and assessment of sensory integration, and it discusses interpretation of assessment data, leading to intervention planning.

Chapter 5, Intervention, addresses the needs of parents, the importance of modifying the sensory environment, and the nature of clinical reasoning during direct intervention. This chapter then provides intervention guidelines with accompanying case studies for children with hyperreactivity, hyporeactivity, and dyspraxia.

Figures, tables, appendices, and references for further study throughout the book are designed to complement the introduction to sensory integration that the text of this monograph provides.

CHAPTER ONE

Sensory Systems and Sensory Integration

A bell rings softly, and baby Abby experiences a sense of pleasure that alerts her and produces a turn toward where the sound is. Her face expresses her interest. She's anticipating that there will be more. The bell rings again, she expresses more pleasure, more movement, and gurgles in delight. Abby's father imitates her gurgle and rings the bell again.

When baby Benita hears the soft ring of a bell, it feels bad in her ears, bad in her stomach, and it reverberates throughout her nervous system in a jarring and unpleasant way. She turns away from the sound and tenses; the expression on her face is stressed, worried, and close to tears. Benita's mother realizes that if she rings the bell again, Benita is likely to wail in protest and thrash about frenetically. Mother frowns sympathetically, puts the bell aside, and moves quietly to soothe and comfort Benita.

It's not the tinkle of a handbell that baby Carl hears— it's the clang of a firehouse gong, followed by the sirens of a fire truck and an ambulance racing past his apartment building, followed by his brother Donald's all-too-accurate imitation of the siren, followed by almost simultaneous bellows from his mother, father, and grandmother. Carl furrows his brow and starts to whimper, but no one notices in the midst of the furor surrounding Donald, who, as racing ambulance, has knocked over a vase. Carl curls up into a ball, sticks his head into the pillow, and withdraws.

Abby, Benita, and Carl are 4-month-olds. Each baby is taking in information from the senses in a distinct way, and each is attempting to adapt to the environment by regulating his or her behavior. The process of organizing sensation from the body and environment for use is known as sensory integration (Ayres, 1979; Kimball, 1999a). Two important aspects of this deceptively simple definition are important. First, the senses are not interpreted in isolation. Instead, we interpret sensation by integrating and organizing input from many modalities to create meaning. Secondly, as we create meaning, we *use* the sensory input to engage in adaptive interactions with our environment. Sensory integrative concepts offer a way to describe individual differences in sensory tolerances and preferences among children and adults that lead to functional behaviors such as play, learning, or social interaction. When we understand these differences in sensory tolerances and preferences, we are better able to create environments that encourage very young children's development. We are also able to help infants and toddlers manage their reactions to sensation and regulate their own behavior.

Let us now see how children who are somewhat older than Abby, Benita, and Carl differ in their responses to a novel sensory environment—an unfamiliar playground.

Emma, age 3, is eager to visit a special "hippopotamus" playground with the children from her child care classroom and their two caregivers. Arriving at the playground, she watches some older children climb on the huge, hollow cast-iron animals and then progresses to a slide that is similar to one at the child care center. After a few turns on the slide, Emma follows her friend Frankie to the hippopotamuses and climbs into one with him. They giggle as the caregiver pretends to look for them.

Gyorgi, a 3-year-old classmate of Emma, holds his primary caregiver's hand on the walk to the new playground, looks somewhat warily at the hippopotamuses, and heads for the sandbox, where he digs and buries toys for 10 minutes. Tanya, his primary caregiver, comes over to comment on Gyorgi's efforts and invites him to inspect a hippopotamus. Gyorgi willingly accompanies Tanya to the animal, which he pets, just like he pets his neighbor's dog. When Tanya offers to give him a boost onto the hippopotamus' back, Gyorgi accepts her help, but immediately asks to get down again.

Jack, another 3-year-old, ran toward the playground pulling the caregiver's hand. He yelled with delight and darted toward the swing set. With the caregiver pushing the swing, Jack cried for 'Higher and higher, faster and faster." Next, he joined the older children on the merry-go-round and spun in circles until he was getting silly and dizzy. Jack didn't get off the merry-go-round until the caregiver insisted. He then ran up to the top of the hill overlooking the playground and rolled all the way down, crashing into the side of the sandbox with manic glee.

The world of an urban American 3-year-old is complicated. Emma, Gyorgi, and Jack are not babies listening to bells any more. Every day they deal with a wealth of sensory input from the physical and social environments encountered during routines, transitions, and novel experiences at home, in the child care setting, and in the community. As we shall see, a number of factors influence a young child's ability to take in, process, and organize sensory input in order to accomplish the basic tasks of early development—building strong, positive relationships with people and exploring the physical environment through play. In addition, a 3-year-old's world is likely to include a number of important adults. These adults may vary considerably in their sensitivity to individual differences in children and in the time and skills they have available to promote a child's self-regulation and adaptive behavior.

Not too many years ago, few people would have paid much attention to the subtleties of the vignettes we have just presented. Pediatricians and parents have always been very concerned about whether a baby could hear, and parents and other caregivers from the dawn of time have learned how to engage and comfort young infants with very different temperaments. For toddlers and slightly older children, expectations vary. Some families and cultures easily tolerate and accommodate young children's individual differences and preferences. Others strive actively to control young children's behavior, especially in group settings. What recent child development research allows us to do is to better understand the processes that underlie the behavior of infants and young children in the context of their physical and social environments. With greater understanding of individual differences among children, adults, and toddlers, families can find ways to create a balance between the demands of the environment and the child's ability to manage these demands—a balance that will promote healthy development and learning.

One of the most exciting areas of child development research in recent decades concerns individual differences in the way human beings perceive sensation and organize sensory input to meet the challenges of daily living. Researchers and clinicians from a number of disciplines

Recent child development research helps us understand the processes that underlie young children's behavior in the context of their environment.

Table 1.1 Research timeline
Contributions to our thinking about sensory integration from diverse sources

Researcher, Profession, and Contribution

Heidelise Als, *Developmental Psychologist*
• Interdependence of nested systems in behavioral organization of neonates
• Impact of environment

Jean Ayres, *Occuptional Therapist and Neuropsychologist*
• Theory of sensory integration
• Nature of sensory integrative disorder and intervention
• Role of experience in changing sensory reactivity

T. Berry Brazelton, *Pediatrician*
• Importance of regulation of state organization and self-calming in neonates

---

Stella Chess, *Psychiatrist*
• Definition and nature of temperament and individual differences
• Concept of goodness-of-fit

Wendy Coster, *Occupational Therapist and Developmental Psychologist*
• Importance of context to function
• Integration of multiple levels of assessment in understanding disability and development

---

Winnie Dunn, *Occupational Therapist*
• Behavioral profiles of sensory integrative disorders
• Connection of neuroscience with sensory integration

Eleanor Gibson, *Developmental Psychologist*
• Role of exploration in development
• The nature of affordances

Peter Gorski, *Neonatologist*
• Environmental effects on neonatal behavior

Stanley Greenspan, *Psychiatrist*
• Affective link to sensory processing
• Functional emotional stages of development

Jerome Kagan, *Developmental Psychologist*
• Clarification of extremes in temperament

Claire Kopp, *Developmental Psychologist*
• Developmental sequence of self-regulation

Barry Lester, *Developmental Psychologist*
• Behavioral expression of infant self-regulation in terms of the "four A's"

Mary Rothbart, *Developmental Psychologist*
• Neurophysiological model of temperament

Daniel Stern, *Psychiatrist*
• Somatosensory contributions to early attachment

Serena Wieder, *Clinical Psychologist*
• Intervention strategies for regulatory disorders

Patricia Wilbarger, *Occupational Therapist*
• Importance of sensory diet for sensory modulation

---

and theoretical orientations have documented these differences. Table 1.1 lists some of the important contributors to our understanding of individual differences in behavioral regulation and sensory processing as they relate to the young child. Their body of research crosses traditional boundaries between scientific disciplines and provides new insights into the functional capacities of children. In this chapter we will link concepts from neuroscience to the theory of sensory integration.

Seven sensory modalities

From early childhood we learn that we have five senses–vision, hearing, touch, taste, and smell. Given an apple, we **see** its red skin, **hear** the crunch as we bite into it, **feel** the chunk in our mouth and the rest of the apple in our hand, **taste** the flavor, and **smell** the freshness. We may concentrate on input from each of these senses, although, more typically, the pleasure in eating an apple comes from an integration of all the senses involved.

As small children, we are taught that we see with our eyes, hear with our ears, touch with our fingers, taste with our tongues, and smell with our noses. In other words, we learn about the basic ways in which we receive sensory input from our external surroundings through specialized sensory receptors. For example, our tongues have specific taste buds that respond to chemicals that are sweet, sour, bitter, and salty, and the retinas in our eyes are sensitive to different types of light that are equivalent to different colors. What we are **not** typically taught are ways to name and think about the unconscious sensory input that comes from our own bodies. There are three main categories of **somatosensation** (from the Greek *somato*—related to the body): tactile, proprioceptive, and vestibular sensations. Everyone knows about the **tactile** or **touch system**. The receptors of the tactile system are imbedded in the skin, which serves as the boundary between the self and the environment. **Proprioception** is the sensation from muscles and joints, resulting from active movement of the body or parts of the body. Proprioception is particularly important to motor development since it is the proprioceptive awareness of our movements that creates the memories necessary for automatic, learned movements like climbing stairs. Finally, the **vestibular system** in the inner ear responds to the movement of the head or head and body in relation to gravity. The vestibular system contributes to our sense of balance and equilibrium as well as movement of the body in space. All three of these somatosensory modalities are intimately involved in the young child's developing sense of self. They influence the ability to interact motorically and emotionally with people and objects. They are also critically important to understanding sensory integration.

The tactile system

The various receptors of the tactile or touch system are imbedded in the skin, which is the largest sensory organ in the body and which covers the entire body and the surface membranes of the internal organs. The tactile system is the first sensory modality to develop in utero and the most mature sensory system at birth (see Figure 1.1) (Kandel, Schwartz & Jessell, 2000; Jacobs, Schneider, & Kraemer, in press; Royeen & Lane, 1991). Many of the newborn's primitive but important approach or avoidance reflexes, such as rooting, cuddling, and withdrawal, are elicited by tactile stimuli.

The tactile system serves two important functions: protection and discrimination. The protective function plays an important role in survival and general tactile awareness of the environment. It is activated by many different stimuli, such as temperature changes of the skin or light touch. The tactile protective component serves a primitive function, but is important throughout life. It is most active during the newborn period and times of extreme stress or threat. It is reciprocally related to a state of arousal and one's feeling about touch. For example, if a child is overtired and irritable, he or she is more likely to interpret a touch as a threat. In contrast, the same touch, when the child is rested and alert, may be an expression of affection or playfulness. One of the most important functions of the protective component is its contribution to the development of attachment between parents and infants (Stern, 1985). For example, as a mother touches and handles her baby during play and nurturing care throughout the day, the baby orients to the touch and usually experiences it as pleasurable. As a result the infant and mother move reciprocally together in a smooth, synchronous give-and-take. Touch provides the foundation for a positive emotional climate. Conversely, during times of threat or stress we

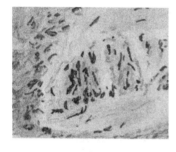

Figure 1.1.
Meisner corpuscles

These receptors, sensitive to touch, consist of encapsulated nerve fibers lying in the skin. A touch on the skin temporarily deforms the capsule causing nerve impulses to send information to the brain.

become extra aware of touch, such as the discomfort one feels when touched on a crowded bus at the end of a busy day ("I am going to jump out of my skin!"). This conceptualization of orienting towards positive touch and withdrawing from or avoiding painful and disorganizing touch is consistent with Als's (1989) work with the premature infant. In these infants, one often sees the balance between approach towards positive touch (e.g., the nurturing security when swaddled and held for a feeding) and the avoidance of negative touch (e.g., the flailing during a medical procedure).

The other important function of the tactile system is discrimination. The tactile discriminative component becomes more developed over time as the child has more experience differentiating various textures, contours, and shapes by touch. We learn discrimination through the integration of deep pressure, light touch, coordinated motion, and precise localization of touch. The fingertips have the highest density of discriminative receptors within the body, but the receptors are found in almost all areas of the skin. Consequently, if we are given an unfamiliar object, we may pinch it (pressure touch) and move it around in our hand to increase discrimination and learn about the object's surface properties, shape, or density. This discriminative capacity is essential for manipulating objects and using them in an adaptive way within the environment.

Of course, the discriminative and protective functions of the tactile system are not completely separate. Some tactile receptors can serve functions of both protection and discrimination. For example, a light touch can promote arousal (protective response) or provide specific information about the texture of a feather (discriminative response). For children who find touch uncomfortable, the protective system predominates and may limit their opportunity to acquire discriminative abilities if it leads to decreased tactile exploration.

The vestibular system

The vestibular system is located in the bony labyrinth of the skull and is attached to the hearing mechanism. It is composed of three structures in the inner ear: the semicircular canals, the saccule, and the utricle. The semicircular canals register the speed, force, and direction of head rotation (e.g., turning your head around to see who is behind

Figure 1.2.
Vestibular system
The labyrinth is composed of the semicircular canals, saccule and utricle. The cochlear is part of the hearing apparatus.

you or spinning on a swing). The saccule and the utricle are sensitive to the force of gravity and linear movement. Figures 1.2, 1.3, and 1.4 illustrate the unique design of these structures. Information from the vestibular system contributes to:

• regulation of muscle tone and coordination (i.e., modifies the readiness of the muscles to act);

• balance and equilibrium;

• ocular-motor control (e.g., controlling eye movements to maintain a stable visual field when moving);

• state of arousal (i.e., maintaining and transitioning between states of alertness or sleep);

• level of attention (i.e., selective maintained focus on what is important); and

• emotional state.

Figure 1.3.
Semicircular canals in the vestibular system
Hair cells are embedded in a gelatinous mass within the canals. Any movement of the head causes the mass to move and therefore deflects the hair cells. Deflection of the hair cells provides information about the speed, force, maintenance, and direction of movement.

Figure 1.4.
Saccule and utricle
Within these chambers are hair cells that are covered by a gelatinous membrane in which calcium crystals are embedded. With head movement, the crystals shift and deflect the hair follicles. Input from these organs provides information regarding the effects of gravity or linear movement.

The vestibular system is quite mature in babies who are born full-term. As the list of functions suggests, the system has a profound effect on the experience of infants, toddlers, and, indeed, all of us. Parents and caregivers learn quickly that gentle, rhythmic rocking tends to soothe a baby and that fast, arrhythmic movements are likely to increase the overall activity level.

Consider the dad who is engaged in roughhouse play with his 9-month-old daughter. He sits on the sofa and bounces her vigorously on his lap. She squeals with delight (high arousal), looks at him intensely (increased attention), and giggles with pleasure (positive emotional

affect). Her muscles tend to tense (increased muscle tone), and she actively balances in sitting (righting and equilibrium reactions). Her visual system and vestibular system work together to inform the child unconsciously whether she is moving, dad is moving, or they are moving together. The vestibular system becomes even more active when the father begins to toss the child in the air over his head. Her response is a general increase in excitability. Before she reaches the point of sensory overload, the dad cradles his daughter in his arms and provides slow rhythmic rocking. This vestibular input, in contrast to the preceding roughhousing, has a calming effect on the baby's arousal and emotional state. She starts to relax, becomes a little sleepy, and feels comforted. Her overall physical tension and muscle tone release. In short order she has progressed from an active alert state to a quiet alert or drowsy state through the influence of vestibular input provided in the context of play.

The proprioceptive system

Proprioceptors are the receptors in the muscles, tendons, and joints that provide information about movement or position of the body in space. Simply put, proprioception is *position sense*—a continuous internal awareness of the posture of the body. For example, when we are sitting on a chair we know without looking whether we are leaning to one side or centered, whether our legs are crossed, whether we are hunched forward or holding ourselves erect, and whether our head is tilted. Proprioception is also *movement sense*—we are aware of when a part of our body is in motion and of its location at all times.

Specifically, proprioception provides information regarding:

• the orientation of the body in space and the relation of body parts to each other;

• the rate and timing of movements as one is moving;

• the force exerted by muscles;

• how much and how fast a muscle is lengthened or shortened during an activity; and

• the changing angles at each joint as we move.

It is important to remember that proprioception tells us about the position and movement of our internal organs, as well as our limbs. For example, when proprio-

Figure 1.5.
Pacinian corpuscles
This proprioceptor, found in the skin and internal organs, is sensitive to pressure. Nerve endings are surrounded by cells arranged concentrically. With pressure on the skin, the concentric circles are temporarily deformed causing sensory information to be relayed to the nervous system.

ceptors known as Pacinian corpuscles (see Figure 1.5) lining the gastric wall are stretched as food enters the stomach, they send signals into the nervous system that make us feel "full" or satiated after a meal.

Proprioception contributes to the development of a *body scheme* or physical sense of self—the internal awareness of body parts, how they relate to the whole, and how they move through space. Proprioception is also central to motor control, since it plays a primary role in how we anticipate and plan movements. It also regulates how we use sensory feedback during and after movement to increase the accuracy of our actions and develop motor skills. Think about picking up a suitcase, for example. If you believe that the suitcase is empty, you will use proprioceptive feedback from prior experiences of picking up empty suitcases to plan your movement. You will "program" enough motor units to fire to give you the force you need to lift a light suitcase. If the suitcase is in fact empty, your feedforward (the planned movement) results in success. If the suitcase is full, the feedforward proprioception will have been inaccurate, leading to an unsuccessful movement that must be modified, based upon both the proprioceptive and visual feedback.

Every sensory modality—those that relate to the external world and somatosensory modalities—has unique properties and serves important functions. While it is useful to discuss each sensory modality in isolation, we seldom experience unimodal sensation in daily life. Rather, it is through our experience of convergence (or integration) of sensation from multiple modalities that we make meaning in the world and learn to master its challenges (Lewkowicz & Lickliter, 1994). As we shall see, the notion of convergence is central to the theory of sensory integration intervention. It argues that we can take advantage of the mutual influence among different sensory modalities to help children overcome problems in modulation or discrimination in any one sensory channel.

Attributes of sensory stimuli

From our brief review of sensory modalities, we know something about the equipment we have available to receive and interpret sensory input from our external surroundings and our bodies. But in order to understand how sensory input is perceived, we must also know something about the stimulus itself. It is helpful to think of two separate entities: *sensory input* (the stimulus itself—a measurable and consistent phenomenon across individuals) and *sensation* or *perception* (the subjective appraisal of sensory input, which varies both within and between individuals). As we have seen, the identical soft ring of a bell can be perceived as a pleasant sensation by one baby and as a disturbing irritant by another. The same touch to the same child can elicit laughter in the morning and tears 15 minutes before supper time. There are three attributes of sensory input in addition to modality that must be considered. These are intensity, duration, and location of input.

Intensity refers to the strength of a stimulus; intensity varies within each modality. Although intensity is a property of the stimulus, it is also dependent upon how it is appraised by each individual. While neuroscience may eventually give us insight into the differences underlying intensity of a sensory input (Kandel, Schwartz, & Jessell, 2000), the response to that input is variable and subjectively appraised within each individual. For example, light touch is more intense than pressure touch (a light touch on the back of one's hand is considerably more intense for most people than a firm touch; a tickle is more intense than a hug). But not all individuals would agree on whether a light touch on the palm of the hand is more intense than a light touch on the face. The difference in how these two sensory inputs are interpreted is more dependent upon the subjective element inherent in the appraisal of that stimulus. The same variability of response is present in all sensory modalities. Rotary vestibular input is more intense than linear (spinning or turning versus up-and-down or side-to-side movement). High-pitched voices are more intense than low-pitched ones. A stable visual stimulus is less intense than a looming stimulus (a banana cream pie in a bakery display case is less intense than a banana cream pie rapidly approaching the face).

Duration is a second important attribute of any sensory stimulus. The concept of duration includes both the duration of the stimulus itself and the duration of the effect of that stimulus in the central nervous system. Duration of the stimulus is easily understood. Consider the light touch described in the preceding paragraph. The touch itself is likely to be brief in duration. However, many people continue to feel the stimulus long after the touch has ended; they may scratch or rub their hand as if to "erase" the input. This aspect of duration is highly variable between, and often within, individuals. It is as if one has to "recover" from the sensory yield of each activity. Generally, the effects of light touch and rotary vestibular input tend to be more lasting than the less intense pressure touch or linear vestibular input. This aspect of sensation contributes to the difficulty many children have at the end of the day (as they are recovering from the cumulative effect of a whole day of sensory inputs) or with transitions between activities.

Location is the final attribute of sensory stimuli. Location refers to the placement of the stimulus on the body or in relation to the body. A light touch on the back of the hand is less intense than one on the palm of the hand, and a light touch on the leg is less intense than a light touch on one's upper lip. Location also influences the ability to modulate sensation. We can interpret a touch or sound whose source we can see more easily than we can interpret a stimulus that comes from behind. An unexpected touch from behind can evoke a flight-or-fight response in many of us.

The process of sensory integration

During the past three decades, researchers and therapists have become increasingly interested in how people perceive and organize information from multiple sensory modalities. As students of development, we have been interested in individual differences in sensory tolerances and preferences among children and adults. As clinicians, we have found that paying close attention to the ways in which young children take in and respond to sensation from multiple modalities deepens our understanding of their behavior and suggests many new ways to help them flourish.

Jean Ayres, an occupational therapist and neuropsychologist, coined the term "sensory integration." Over time, she and her colleagues developed this succinct definition of the term: **Sensory integration is a process that involves organizing sensation from the body and the environment for use** (Ayres, 1979; Fisher, Murray, & Bundy, 1991; Kimball, 1999a, 1999b). Three aspects of this relatively simple definition are important:

• Sensory integration refers to the dynamic processing or **organization** of information from all sensory modalities. Much of the professional literature addressing perception and learning focuses on vision and hearing. In contrast, sensory integration researchers view the more proximal senses of touch, proprioception, and vestibular input as equally important.

• Sensory integrative theory views the integration and **convergence** of input from multiple modalities as essential to learning and performance. Whereas sensory input is usually studied or discussed in terms of a single modality, in reality the central nervous system does not perceive or register sensation as isolated modalities. We rely on mutual influences among different sensory modalities every moment of the day (e.g., our visual, proprioceptive, and vestibular systems work together to stabilize the visual field as we are walking).

• Sensory integration refers to the **active use** of sensory input as the basis for an adaptive response. Passive spinning while enclosed in a net swing may not require sensory integration, while engaging in a playful game of catch while on the swing does. Sensory integrative intervention is not synonymous with passive sensory stimulation, even when enriched sensory experiences are provided. The child must be actively engaged in taking in the sensation and organizing some type of intrinsically motivated action in order to benefit from treatment.

Components of the sensory integrative process

Sensory integration can be thought of as occurring in five sequential steps (see Figure 1.6).

• **Sensory registration**—is the initial awareness of a sensation. It is dependent upon recognizing the novelty of the stimulus: "Something new has happened; I have been touched."

• **Orientation and attention**—we pay selective attention to the stimulus: "I have been touched here, on the arm."

• **Interpretation**—we give meaning to the stimulus: "Uh-oh, it's a mosquito bite." This component is to some extent cognitive, since we interpret new sensation in the light of experience and learning. We also appraise sensation emotionally, in terms of threat, challenge, or pleasure.

• **Organization of a response**—we determine a cognitive, affective, and/or motor response: "Drat—maybe I'll have to go inside to wait for the ice cream truck." This organization is not always cognitive. For example, motor planning occurs before even automatic responses like swatting a mosquito.

• **Execution of the response**—this final step of sensory integration is the only one that can be directly observed. We may make a comment that reflects a cognitive response: "I should have brought the insect repellent." We may convey affect with a grimace or exclamation: "Mosquito bites give me the willies!" Our response may be motoric: a slap on the arm. If the execution involves a motor act, then new sensory input is generated and the cycle begins again.

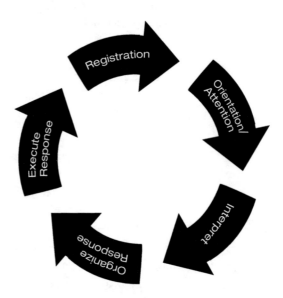

Figure 1.6.
The five components of the sensory integrative process.

While this sequence makes intuitive sense, actual sensory processing is much more complex than this discussion would imply and occurs much too rapidly for one to be aware of it. In addition, whereas this sequence suggests a simple linear process, that is not the way interaction with the environment actually occurs. At any moment many different types of sensation are at multiple stages of processing.

Summary

Sensory integration involves organizing sensation from the body and the environment for adaptive use. This process occurs in five steps—registration, orientation and attention, interpretation, organization of a response, and execution of that response. When thinking of the sensation that supports sensory integration, one must pay particular attention to the somatosensory systems (i.e., touch, proprioceptive and vestibular). In addition, one must consider how sensation is perceived by each individual. Subjective perception depends on three attributes of the stimulus—intensity, duration, and location. This introduction to sensory systems provides a foundation for looking at the behavior that results from the processes of sensory integration and for thinking about the sensory bases of self-regulation.

CHAPTER TWO

Observing Sensory-Based Behavior in Infants and Young Children in Context

This chapter focuses on the observable behavior that results from sensory processing. It provides a framework for understanding how the sensory integrative process is revealed in the behavior of infants and young children within the context of their physical and social environments. Anyone who spends time with more than one baby or toddler, or who spends significant amounts of time with one small child, quickly becomes aware of individual differences in patterns of behavior among children and of considerable variations in any single child's capacity for self-regulation. All too frequently, however, adults find themselves caught up in trying to *manage* young children's behavior before they *understand* it. As we shall see, the poorly adaptive or challenging behaviors in many children may have their roots in difficulties with sensory processing. Since sensory integration is invisible, we must learn how to observe behavior that will tell us how a child processes sensory information and manages environmental challenges. We must learn to recognize clues to the sensory basis for a child's behavior, for these will suggest intervention approaches that are likely to promote a child's learning and performance.

The "four A's" of infancy

Barry Lester and his colleagues, who first gained recognition through their meticulous descriptive studies of patterns of infant crying, provide a useful set of lenses for focusing on the observable behavior that results from infants' sensory processing (Lester, Freier, & LaGasse, 1995). The four A's of infancy describe the principal ways in which infants and toddlers perceive and modulate sensory information.

Arousal, **attention**, **affect**, and **action** form the core of behavioral regulation in the young child. As Figure 2.1 suggests, each of the "four A's" is a reflection of sensory integration. Each of the "four A's" requires self-regulation. For example, we regulate our state of arousal as we wake up in the morning and get ready for the day by making a transition from a sleep state to a more alert state, which we maintain for most of the day. In addition, within each A, each of the "four A" processes has a mutual regulatory influence on the other processes. Thus a child's ability to regulate arousal allows him to focus and maintain attention and to organize action. This type of integration is similar to the synactive organization in the neonate described by Als (1989). The synactive system of development is a nested conceptualization of neonatal behavioral

Figure 2.1
The mutual regulatory influence on the four A's

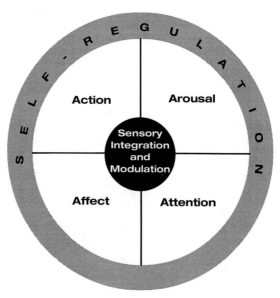

regulation in which four different processes are interdependent and mutually influencing. The four systems are physiology, state, motor, and attentional/interactive. Physiological regulation is at the core and is the focus of most medical interventions in the neonate. It is surrounded by the increasingly more complex processes of state, motor, and attentional/interactive systems. They contribute more complex interactions between the neonate and the environment, eventually enabling the child to interact socially. Our conceptualization of sensory-based self-regulation differs from Als's (1986) in that we do not propose a nested system in which arousal is at the core—rather each of these processes contributes equally to behavioral organization.

Arousal refers to the infant's ability to maintain alertness and make transitions between different states of sleep and wakefulness. Berg and Berg (1979) and Brazelton (1984) were among the first to identify and describe six distinct states among newborns: deep sleep, light sleep, drowsy, quiet alert (full attention with no body movement), active alert (less attentive to external stimuli with body movement), and crying. Among high-risk newborns, difficulty in regulating state behavior (i.e., alternating between different states smoothly) is often one of the first signs of problems, and improvement in state regulation is one of the earliest signs of recovery (Als, 1989). The need to observe a child's state of arousal, however, does not end with the neonatal period. State of arousal continues to influence (and be influenced by) children's perceptions and interpretations of sensory input long after they attain stable sleep-wake patterns. For example, the physical handling and movement that may be acceptable to a toddler during a drowsy or quiet alert state may be interpreted as aversive when the child is stressed or in an active alert state. As adults, we experience the same phenomenon. Think about walking on a dark city street late at night. Your state of arousal may be heightened, and a light touch would be interpreted as a threat and elicit a fight-or-flight response. In contrast, the same touch occurring when you are at home in a drowsy state might elicit a calm, orienting response instead of a negative reaction. In clinical practice, it is important to take a child's state of arousal into account. During an assessment, for example, a child's state of arousal is usually heightened. An examiner must be careful to interpret a child's reactivity to sensation in the

Arousal—
the infant's ability to maintain alertness and make transitions between states.

context of the child's initial state of arousal and subsequent changes in that state as the assessment progresses.

Attention is the ability to focus selectively on a desired stimulus or task. Most children are able to sustain focused attention most easily in a quiet alert state. However, children who are described as typically "busy" and active may attend best in an active alert state. Many factors contribute to the ability to attend and the quality of that attention. Most important are the ability to maintain an appropriate level of alertness, selection (i.e., choosing what to attend to and the ability to shift between several foci), and allocation (i.e., the amount of time a child can attend to a stimulus and the amount of effort inherent in maintaining that focus). When thinking about attention from a sensory perspective, it is also critical to recognize that children may have a preference for certain modalities. One child may calm and orient to a visual target, while another will calm and orient to a music box or her mother's voice.

It is not unusual for a young child who is having sensory integrative or self-regulatory problems to be able to attend to input in only one modality at a time. If two or more sensory modalities are combined, behavioral disorganization may occur. This is particularly common in very young infants. For example, some infants may be able to smile and look at their parent only if the parent does not speak; when an auditory stimulus is combined with the visual one, the baby may become over-stimulated and unable to maintain attention.

Sensory modulation, the ability to manage reaction to sensation (described more fully in Chapter 3), influences young children's capacity for sustaining focused attention. Some children, easily over-stimulated and hypervigilant, may actively avoid sensory input. For example, one child may actively avert her gaze during face-to-face social interaction; another may hide under the table during free play in a toddler group. In contrast, a child who requires a lot of intense sensory input in order to notice the environment may be inattentive and nonresponsive in many quiet situations, since he or she has not yet oriented to salient stimuli in the environment.

Affect is the emotional component of behavior. One can understand the relation between sensation and emotion on two levels. First, sensation often elicits an emotional reaction, which tells us a great deal about how the child is subjectively appraising a specific sensory experi-

Attention—
the ability to focus selectively on a desired stimulus or task.

ence. Think, for example, about the child who laughs while on a rapidly moving swing or, in contrast, the child who cries in apparent terror after hearing an unexpected noise. Secondly, affect is also inherent in social relationships, which involve sensations. For example, the interaction between a mother and her child often involves gentle touch, while active peer play may involve proprioception and vestibular input. If a child cannot tolerate these sensations, relationships may be disrupted (Holloway, 1998).

Affect—
the emotional component of behavior.

Children who have difficulty managing their reactions to sensation (sensory modulation) often have atypical, heightened, or depressed affective responses to sensory input. Such difficulty is of particular concern in very young children, because their unusual responses to sensation can influence the formation of primary attachment relationships (Stern, 1985). Consider Julie, an infant who is irritable and tactually defensive (i.e., perceives touch as aversive); she stiffens when held or cuddled. Julie's mother is afraid that Julie "doesn't like her." In response, she tends to leave Julie alone and calm rather than disrupting her tenuous equilibrium by offering interaction and additional sensory input. As a result, Julie and her mother have few opportunities for important nurturing and reciprocal social interaction. If this pattern continues over time, the attachment relationship between mother and child may be in jeopardy.

Some children who have difficulty organizing sensations from the body and the environment develop characteristic behavioral patterns that may interfere with their ability to explore and form relationships (Ayres, 1972; ZERO TO THREE, 1994). They may not develop the wide range and depth of affective expression that is appropriate for their age or may exhibit unusual patterns of anxiety that can be traced to sensory modulation disorders (Koomar, 1996). Young children who have problems in sensory modulation may have a hard time being playful. Playfulness is the ability to suspend reality in order to "pretend" and enjoy one's self during flexible play (Bundy, 1991). Such children may find it difficult to be playful for two reasons. First, they may feel anxious during play situations and therefore watch or withdraw from the action. Secondly, they may actively avoid the sensory input that is so much a part of most young children's play.

Action, the final "A," is the ability to engage in adaptive goal-directed behavior (Anzalone, 1993). It involves

Action—
the ability to engage in adaptive, goal-directed behavior.

organizing perception and cognition in order to behave with a purpose. Although motor abilities are the foundation for action, action is much more complex than movement alone. Muscle tone, postural reflexes, strength, and skill are aspects of neuromotor maturation that are necessary to engage in action. Play is a good example of action that is dependent upon neuromotor maturation but that is much more than just motor coordination. In order to play successfully, a child must be able to form a goal for action that is based in the environment and be able to sequence a series of actions in order to bring about the effects he or she desires. For example, a toddler envisions a train and lines up his small trucks to make the cars of the train. He then carefully pushes the "train" up a mountain made out of sofa cushions as he makes whistle sounds. In this view, action depends upon the interaction between the child and the environment.

Sensory-related behavior in the context of the environment: Goodness-of-fit

It should be clear from the preceding discussion that we cannot understand young children's sensory-related behavioral organization by observing them in isolation. Rather, we must study children's abilities within the context of their physical and social environments. The physical environment includes the objects and spaces that children experience in their daily life. Ideally, it offers opportunities and challenges for exploration as well as the sense of safety and security that is essential for learning. From a sensory perspective, we can judge the physical environment as a potential source of sensory input that is either calming or arousing. For example, natural lighting and sound-absorbing materials in a child care center help organize sensory input for young children. In contrast, a harshly lit, noisy, chaotic setting heightens arousal and possibly disorganization. As we have seen, heightened arousal makes it difficult for most children to focus their attention.

The social environments important to babies and young children encompass caregiving relationships, parental style, and the ability of the social partner to modulate interaction based on the infant's communicative cues. While we are used to thinking about social aspects of relationships that contribute to cognitive and emotional development, we should also think about the social contributors to sensory integration. Caregivers and other people are a major source of sensory input. For instance, an attuned caregiver may hold an infant with a secure gentleness, a quiet smile, and a firm pressure touch. The child responds with comfort and organization of the "four A's." A caregiver who is not as good an observer of a child's reactivity may be too loud or touch too much. As a result, the child may be over-stimulated or dysregulated.

The concept of **goodness-of-fit** offers a useful way to think about young children's sensory-related behavior in their physical and social environments. Alexander Thomas and Stella Chess (1977) introduced the concept of goodness-of-fit in their pioneering study of temperamental differences among children. Goodness-of-fit refers to the match between a child's needs and abilities and the demands and supports of the environment. This concept is also helpful when thinking about sensory integration. When there is a good fit between a child's sensory integrative capacities and the demands of the physical and social environments, the child achieves balanced self-regulation. Indeed it is the mutual regulation between the child and caregiver over time that helps the child to learn self-regulation in response to environmental changes. Goodness-of-fit does not imply a challenge-free or unusually protected environment. Rather, goodness-of-fit describes a situation of a just right or optimal challenge, which promotes learning and development (Chess & Thomas, 1986; Zeitlin & Williamson, 1994).

The story of Madeline

The story of Madeline and her mother illustrates the interaction between an infant's intrinsic capacities for self-regulation and sensory modulation and the external physical and social environment (see Figure 2.2). Madeline was born at 34 weeks gestation; her corrected age is now 3 months. Linda, her mother, describes Madeline as a quiet, independent baby, who is somewhat irritable and not very affectionate. We observed Madeline and Linda during a brief social play period. The observation focuses on their interaction in terms of the "four A's" and the sensory experiences of Madeline.

Madeline was in an infant seat on a low table, facing her mother. Initially, she was in a quiet alert state of arousal

Figure 2.2
Interaction of Madeline and her mother

with a wide-eyed expression and little movement of her arms and legs. Linda, sitting on the edge of her chair, with shoulders hunched, seemed somewhat tense. When Linda dangled a set of plastic keys a few inches from Madeline's face, Madeline focused briefly but then averted her gaze. She furrowed her brow, the movements of her arms and legs became jerky, and she began to cry. Linda tried different methods to comfort Madeline—talking to her, wiping her mouth, and rocking her in the infant seat. Madeline cried more vigorously. After a few minutes, Linda pulled back, frustration evident in her facial expression, defeated posture, and silence. When her mother was quiet, Madeline became calmer. She began to look at Linda's face and smile. She slowed down the movements of her arms and legs, began to bring her hands together in midline, even tried to suck on her fingers, and eventually smiled at Linda.

Madeline was capable of self-regulation of arousal, attention, affect, and action. But she could self-regulate only when the environment was relatively quiet. Linda's effort to engage Madeline with the keys and her subsequent attempts to comfort Madeline increased the sensory input that the baby had to manage—and she could not handle it.

What happened next revealed the pattern of interaction that was becoming established between mother and daughter. When Madeline smiled at her, Linda responded enthusiastically, beginning to talk to and touch her daughter. Madeline tried to maintain the interaction by using her limited abilities at self-regulation. She looked briefly away from her mother, and then looked back, and finally sucked on her fingers. Unfortunately these attempts were not effective in maintaining Madeline's behavioral organization in the face of Linda's efforts. For as Madeline looked away, Linda tried to maintain engagement by giving her more verbal cues and by bringing her face into Madeline's visual field. What was happening was that Linda's attempts at nurturing and capturing her daughter's attention were increasing the sensory input that Madeline was trying to manage. Eventually, Madeline could no longer maintain attempts at self-regulation and resumed crying—becoming the irritable child her mother had described to us.

Understanding Madeline's capacity for sensory-based self-regulation provided the key to understanding the relationship between this baby and mother and to helping them achieve a warm, attuned relationship. We could see that Madeline was capable of engaging in social interaction, but only if the environment was relatively quiet and calm. When the environment became too complex and over-stimulating for her, she would attempt to use self-regulatory strategies to "manage" the stimulation, but she could not succeed for long. There was a good fit between Linda and Madeline during relatively quiet times. But when Linda became more stimulating, the sensory demands of social interaction exceeded Madeline's resources for managing them. Linda was a loving, nurturing, and intelligent mother, but she had difficulty reading Madeline's subtle cues and therefore unintentionally overloaded her baby with sensory input. When we reviewed a videotape of this session with Linda, she was moved to tears as she realized that Madeline's smile was meant for her, and she recognized her daughter's heroic efforts to maintain a connection. Over time Linda was able to modulate her own behavior, talk with her husband and other family members about Madeline's needs, and create the tranquil physical environment that her daughter needed at this stage in her development.

Summary

This chapter introduces the "four A's"—arousal, attention, affect and action—which can be seen as the behavioral expression of an infant or young child's sensory integration. The "four A's" provide a framework for observing and describing sensory-based self-regulation. The concept of goodness-of-fit offers a useful way to think about young children's sensory-related behavior in their physical and social environments. A goal of sensory integrative intervention is to establish a goodness-of-fit between sensory demands of the physical and social environments and the resources of the child to manage them.

CHAPTER THREE

Patterns of Sensory Integration

In this monograph, we discuss the sensory integration and self-regulation of very young children across the developmental continuum, from infants and toddlers who are developing typically to those with severe difficulties. This chapter introduces two aspects of sensory integrative functioning that influence a child's position on that continuum. These are:

• **Sensory modulation**—the ability to manage reaction to sensation, best described in terms of a **threshold** to sensory input; and

• **Praxis**—the ability to use sensory input as the foundation for formulating goals, planning and sequencing novel actions.

The concepts of sensory modulation and praxis allow us to describe different behavioral patterns of young children who have difficulties with sensory processing. These patterns, along with the "four A's," will provide a context for our discussion of sensory integrative assessment, in Chapter 4, and intervention, in Chapter 5.

This chapter also includes a discussion of two diagnostic categories in ZERO TO THREE's system of classifying mental health and developmental disorders in infants and young children (ZERO TO THREE, 1994). This system, which focuses on affective, behavioral, and relational problems, includes two major diagnostic categories that reflect problems in sensory integration—regulatory disorders and multisystem developmental disorders (disorders of relating and communicating).

Sensory modulation and sensory threshold

As we observed 3-month-old Madeline (Chapter 2), we saw that she could regulate her arousal, attention, affect, and action to some degree. But when she was faced with intense sensory input from multiple modalities, she could not maintain that regulation. Madeline's mother recognized that there was something unusual about the way her daughter reacted to her efforts to engage and comfort her, but she did not attribute that to sensation. Feeling rejected by her baby, Linda described Madeline as "irritable" and "not very affectionate." If Linda had not learned to see her daughter's behavior as a response to sensory overload rather than a rejection of her nurturance, their relationship might have been in serious jeopardy.

Madeline's story is not that unusual and illustrates the individual variability in reaction to sensory input that is central to understanding sensory integration. The ability to manage and organize reaction to sensation in a graded and adaptive way is referred to as sensory modulation. **Sensory modulation** is a process that occurs on both a neurophysiological level and a behavioral level (McIntosh, Miller, Shyu & Hagerman, 1999). For the purpose of this discussion, we will discuss the behavioral level. Sensory modulation is related to the sensory registration step of the sensory integrative process that was discussed in Chapter One (Ayres, 1972). Three different factors are important in understanding sensory modulation: sensory threshold, the rate of recovery from sensation, and the amount of time a child can remain in an optimal zone of responsivity.

When thinking about sensory modulation, it is important to consider the sensory threshold, or point of initial responsivity to sensory input (Dunn, 1997, 1999). **Sensory threshold** varies both between and within individuals. In most of us, this threshold is high enough that we can tolerate the complexity and stimulation inherent in the environment, yet low enough that we can perceive subtle changes and novelty in the environment. When a child is functioning below this threshold, the child is inattentive to the ambient sensory input. That is, the child has not yet noticed any change or novelty in the sensory environment. Sensory threshold does not describe a discrete, stationary point where a stimulus of a given intensity, duration, or frequency is detected (Anzalone & Williamson, 2000;

Dunn, 1997; Wilbarger & Wilbarger, 1991). When thinking of sensory threshold, we are not talking about the discrete perception of a single sensory input in a single modality (e.g., the detection of a high-frequency sound or visual acuity). Rather, we are referring to the central process through which input from multiple sensory modalities is combined (or summed) over time and space. It is variable within the individual and influenced by many factors, including the accumulation of sensation over time, the type and intensity of sensation, the rate of recovery from each stimulus (i.e., the duration of effect as opposed to the duration of the stimulus), the child's pre-existing internal state of arousal and previous sensory experiences, and the child's motivation. The outcome of this summation is not discrimination but alertness, attention, and to some extent a sense of emotional well-being. What sensation enables an individual to do is to attain and sustain an optimal level of arousal. Sensory threshold helps us to understand how much sensation it takes to *attain* that level of arousal, but it is also important to consider the child's ability to *sustain* that level of arousal.

The ability to sustain optimal arousal is also variable. Once most of us attain optimal arousal, we are able to engage in adaptive action and maintain the arousal with ongoing sensory input. That area of optimal arousal can be thought of as a zone. Ideally, we have a wide zone that enables us to take in more sensory input as we engage in adaptive behavior and recover from past sensory experiences. For example, think of Elliot, a toddler, who is engaged in roughhouse play with his father. Elliot is laughing as his father tickles him all over his body (high intensity tactile), sings his favorite song (low intensity auditory), and randomly kisses him all over his face (high intensity visual and tactile). This level of positive interaction is sustained with both father and son laughing happily. When Elliot is picked up for a final "raspberry" on his belly (high intensity vestibular and tactile), however, he is somewhat frightened and stops laughing to take a deep breath. His father notes Elliot's pause and gives him a break before resuming his song. What Elliot's father perceived was that, while Elliot could attain an optimal state of arousal for playful social interaction, that zone was not infinite. Elliot could get over-stimulated and over-excited when too much sensory or different input was provided. Sensitive observation enabled the father to quickly re-enter the zone

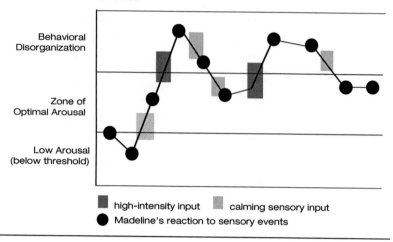

Figure 3.1

Madeline's shifts in arousal and behavioral organization as a result of changes in sensory events

Behavioral Disorganization

Zone of Optimal Arousal

Low Arousal (below threshold)

■ high-intensity input ▨ calming sensory input
● Madeline's reaction to sensory events

by slowing down the flow of sensation and providing some time for recovery.

Our observations of Madeline, discussed earlier, illustrate the variability of sensory threshold within an individual. During her interaction with her mother, Madeline was receiving tactile, auditory, vestibular, and visual inputs over time. At the beginning of her interaction, she was able to attend to her mother briefly but could not sustain the attention and interaction. Although Madeline was easily overwhelmed by the build up of stimuli, she tried hard to orient and attend to her mother's face and voice—her motivation helped her behavioral organization. Madeline was better able to regulate her attention after a period of quiet. The quiet allowed her to recover and return to her optimal state of arousal. Wilbarger and Wilbarger (1991) provide a conceptualization of sensory modulation that is helpful in understanding what Madeline is experiencing. Figure 3.1 illustrates an interaction between Madeline and her mother from a sensory perspective. The shaded rectangles in the figure represent accumulated sensory events of varying modalities and intensities. As she experienced these events, Madeline quickly reached her initial threshold, which is somewhat low. The figure also illustrates the ongoing sensory events to which she was reacting. These additional events continued to influence her arousal, and she moved from an optimal level of arousal into a zone of over-arousal and behavioral disorganization. What is apparent from this schematic is that the accumulation of sensation was too fast for Madeline. Because she was unable to recover from the sensory input that her mother provided for her, she quickly entered her zone of optimal arousal and just as quickly moved out of it into behavioral disorganization and affective unavailability. When the flow of sensation slowed down, however, Madeline was readily able to exhibit her self-regulatory behaviors and interact with her mother.

As noted, sensory modulation is variable both within and between individuals. Generally, that variability is not of clinical concern—it is merely part of what makes each of us unique individuals. Both Elliot and Madeline have unique profiles of sensory modulation. Both of them, however, are able to recover independently. This is not always the case. In some children who are unable to moderate their responses to ongoing sensory events, sensory modulation can become problematic. We should talk in terms of dysfunction only when a child stays in the extreme ranges of threshold or when a child has a very narrow zone of optimal arousal. In these children the sensory modulation problems interfere with self-regulation and the ability to participate in desirable age-appropriate activities. Figure 3.2 illustrates two distinct categories along a continuum of sensory reactivity from low to high threshold. Children at the extremes of the continuum are either easily over-stimulated, or they are frequently under-stimulated (Anzalone & Williamson, 2000; Dunn, 1997; Williamson & Anzalone, 1997). Another pattern of dysfunction is seen when there is a very narrow zone of optimal arousal in which the child cannot maintain focused arousal and attention. While we are describing sensory modulation in terms of observable behavior in this monograph, there is an underlying neurophysiological basis of

Figure 3.2
Continuum of sensory threshold reactivity

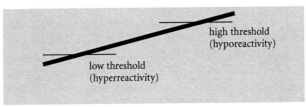

high threshold
(hyporeactivity)

low threshold
(hyperreactivity)

this behavior (McIntosh, Miller, Shyu, & Hagerman, 1999).

Children with very low thresholds do not require much sensory input before they detect it and activate their nervous systems. Like Madeline, they may easily be over-stimulated by their experiences or environments. These children are frequently referred to as *sensory-defensive* or *over-responders* and have received a good deal of attention from researchers and clinicians (Ayres, 1979; Knickerbocker, 1980; Wilbarger & Wilbarger 1991). At the opposite end of the continuum are children with a high threshold. They may appear to be disengaged, disinterested, or flat in affect. The sensory input available in most environments is not enough to reach the sensory threshold of these children. Clearly, children who do not register sensation will not be able to proceed with subsequent steps in sensory processing. Often, as a result of their seeming passivity, these children elicit *less* stimulation from both the physical and social environments while requiring *more*. Children at either end of the threshold continuum often have difficulty regulating reactivity to support the organization of arousal, attention, affect, and action.

Sensory modulation profiles

The concepts of sensory threshold and the zone of optimal arousal help us to recognize a child's capacity for sensory modulation in a specific situation and over time, but the concept of sensory threshold does not completely explain children's sensory-based behavior. We must also recognize that, in order to cope with internal and external demands, some children act in accordance with their sensory threshold while others attempt to compensate for it (Anzalone & Williamson, 2000; Dunn, 1997, 1999). Table 3.1 describes the interaction between sensory threshold and behavioral response. The child with a low threshold who acts in accordance with his threshold will be hyperreactive; this pattern is typically seen in children with auditory, visual, movement, tactile, or sensory defensiveness. However, some children with sensory defensiveness attempt to compensate for their low threshold and "manage" over-arousal by avoiding sensory input. These children are less likely than others to engage in exploratory play, for example. Each of these profiles is characterized by a distinct behavioral pattern that can be described in terms of the "four A's."

Table 3.1
Sensory modulation profiles

	LOW (Increased Sensitivity)	HIGH (Decreased Sensitivity)
Acts in accordance with threshold	Hyperreactive	Hyporeactive
Attempts to counteract threshold	Sensory Avoider	Sensory Seeker

(Modified from Dunn, 1999)

Children who are **hyperreactive** (i.e., low threshold and acting in accordance with their threshold) have a high level of **arousal**. They are easily overwhelmed by the sensory input generated by daily living and are usually over-aroused and stressed. Their **attention** is unfocused, and they are often described as distractible. This distractibility derives from their inability to "screen out" irrelevant input. Their **affective** state is often negative or stressed and fearful. These children may not look toward adults or other children for interaction since social relationships often create unpredictable and unwanted sensory input. Thus their **actions** are often defensive or protective in nature and may appear to be impulsive.

Children who are **sensory avoiders** (i.e., low threshold and compensating for their threshold) are seemingly aware of their sensory needs. They actively avoid sensory input in order to manage their low threshold and protect themselves from over-stimulation. These children are often, but not always, able to modulate their **arousal** level. When they are successful at avoiding sensory input, they succeed at maintaining a calm and alert state. Their **attention**, however, is hypervigilant—they must constantly attend to stimuli in the environment in order to avoid unexpected sensation. Consequently, these children, while aware of stimuli in the environment, are not necessarily attending to those stimuli considered salient by adults. They may be focusing on stimuli that adults consider irrelevant, such as the feel of labels on their clothing, the sound of traffic on the street, the accidental touch of a passing person, or the flickering of a fluorescent light. The **affect** of sensory-avoidant children is often fearful or anxious. They are frequently described as controlling, since one way of avoiding sensation is to attempt to prevent the unexpected from occurring. Finally, these children tend to be passive or unengaged in **action**. They have learned that environmental exploration can yield undesirable sensory input. The effect of active sensory avoidance on subsequent development is important to consider. Children who try to limit encountering sensation often miss out on learning experiences.

Children who are **hyporeactive** have a high threshold, requiring a lot of sensory input before responding. Hyporeactive children who act according to their threshold tend to have decreased **arousal**, since they often do not register the opportunities for interaction in their surroundings. They have a latency in **attending** to the environment since it takes so much input for them to achieve threshold. In groups, these children often notice opportunities to join in play only after peers have moved on to other activities or more receptive children. **Affect** is often restricted in these children, who are seldom meaningfully engaged with either the physical or social environments. Although hyporeactive children are sometimes described as looking sad or uninterested, this is often not the case. In reality, they simply have not yet achieved threshold, and have not yet noticed opportunities for action. As a result, they are passive or slow to take **action**. It is important to note that affective engagement and adaptive action in all infants and young children depends to some extent upon emotional reciprocity with adult caregivers. Children who are hyporeactive are quiet; they do not exhibit the types of cues that adults expect from children who are receptive to interaction. Consequently, these children elicit *less* interaction (with the resulting decrease in sensory input) from adults, although what they need is *more* social engagement.

Children who are **sensory seekers** also have a high threshold, but, unlike hyporeactive children, they actively attempt to meet their need for a high level of sensory input. Since these children try hard to achieve and maintain alertness, their **arousal** is heightened, but it is likely to be inconsistent. These children may become over-aroused just as often as optimally aroused. They are able to engage in activities necessary to achieve threshold but do not stop there. They often continue to engage in intensive sensory experiences and, therefore, pass right through their optimal zone of arousal into a state of behavioral disorganization (see Figure 3.1). Because of their inconsistent arousal level, **attention** in sensory seekers is often poorly modulated. In addition, what sensory seekers attend to is often not what adults in their environment may consider salient. These children are much more likely to pay attention to the "sensory yield" in their surroundings (e.g., the thrill of climbing to the top of a bookcase) than to the environment's learning potential (e.g., reading the books in the bookcase). **Affect** is variable among sensory seekers. If they can meet their sensory needs, affect is differentiated and appropriate. However, when sensory needs are not met, their affect resembles the flat, uninvested demeanor of the child with hyporeactivity. **Action** may cause problems for sensory seekers. In their efforts to obtain sensory input, they may engage in impulsive or risky behavior. As adolescents or adults, sensory seekers often indulge in high-risk, high-sensory sports such as "extreme skiing" or football.

Table 3.2 summarizes the behavioral expression of the "four A's" within each of the sensory profiles we have described. These sensory profiles provide valuable insight into behavior and help us to plan intervention. However, they are not mutually exclusive. Some children may not consistently fit into any one profile. Others may exhibit a combination of behaviors that cut across a number of categories or exhibit different patterns in different sensory modalities (e.g., be hyperreactive to touch and sensory-seeking of vestibular input).

In work with very young children, it is particularly important to distinguish between children who are sensory avoidant and children who are hyporeactive. Children in each of these categories may appear flat and unavailable for interaction with the environment, yet they are unavailable for very different reasons. When a very young child appears withdrawn, the wisest initial strategy is to *decrease* environmental sensory input. Children who are hyporeactive will not exhibit much behavioral change with decreased sensory stimulation. However, children who are sensory avoidant may become more organized when sensory input is decreased. Once one identifies the child's pattern of sensory modulation and understands whether he is acting in accordance with, or to compensate for, his sensory threshold, one can formulate an appropriate, individualized intervention plan to help a child cope successfully with sensory dysfunction.

Table 3.2

Sensory profiles expressed in terms of the "four A's"

Arousal

Hyperreactive (low threshold)	Usually high arousal
Sensory Avoidant (low threshold)	Attempts to modulate arousal, so is often in a quiet state
Hyporeactive (high threshold)	Usually decreased arousal
Sensory Seeking (high threshold)	Arousal may be heightened, but labile

Attention

Hyperreactive (low threshold)	Inability to focus attention; distractible
Sensory Avoidant (low threshold)	Hypervigilant, since needs to "scan" for sensory threats
Hyporeactive (high threshold)	Inattentive or has a latency to attend; often misses interactional opportunities because of latency
Sensory Seeking (high threshold)	Poorly modulated attention that focuses on strongest sensory input, not learning

Affect

Hyperreactive (low threshold)	Predominantly negative affect
Sensory Avoidant (low threshold)	Fearful or anxious; when older, may be demanding
Hyporeactive (high threshold)	Restricted or flat affect; may appear depressed
Sensory Seeking (high threshold)	Affect is variable, but may become over-excited with excess sensory input

Action

Hyperreactive (low threshold)	Impulsive reactions; may seem aggressive
Sensory Avoidant (low threshold)	Constrained; avoids developmentally appropriate exploration
Hyporeactive (high threshold)	Passive; may watch action but not engage
Sensory Seeking (high threshold)	Action is geared primarily to gaining sensation; may be impulsive and take risks

Praxis and dyspraxia

While sensory modulation is one important aspect of sensory integration, it is not the only component that is important in evaluating and assisting young children with sensory integrative dysfunction. Sensory modulation profiles help us to understand differences in the way children register sensory input, orient or attend to it, and interpret it (the first three components of sensory integration). But we must also understand the difficulties children experience in *using* the sensory input they obtain from their body or from the environment. The concept of **praxis** is central to this effort. Praxis is the ability to conceptualize, organize, and direct unfamiliar purposeful action (Ayres, 1985; Cermak, 1991). Praxis is central to action as defined in the "four A's" framework. The difference between **praxis** and **action** is that praxis has to do with *novel* action, whereas "four A's" action could also be familiar action.

Praxis involves the planning and sequencing of novel motor acts. It is a bridge between cognition and motor abilities and encompasses the final two steps of the sensory integrative process—the organization and execution of a response to sensory input. Praxis depends upon, but is not synonymous with, motor ability. According to Ayres, "praxis is to the physical world what language is to the social; it enables interaction" (Ayres, 1985, p. 1).

Praxis encompasses three interdependent steps:

• ideation (formulating the goal for action based upon perception of what is possible in the environment;

• motor planning (figuring out specifically how to accomplish the goal through problem solving, sensorimotor awareness of the body, and sequencing actions); and

• execution (actually carrying out the planned action).

Adequate sensory integration is required for all steps of praxis. For example, in order to form a goal, a child must notice and orient to novelty and be motivated to explore the environment. If a child perceives the environment as over-stimulating and threatening, she will be more likely to avoid the environment than to explore it. Similarly, if a child cannot optimally process the tactile and proprioceptive feedback he obtains from motor activities, he will not develop a body scheme that is adequate to support motor planning and the development of motor skills.

Ideation, the first step of praxis, establishes the goal for action. Ideation is the ability to discover the possibilities for action in the environment; it is the most clearly cognitive aspect of praxis. In contrast, **motor planning**, the second step of praxis, is the most clearly sensory component. Motor planning is the process of figuring out how to accomplish a goal that involves sequential actions. It is dependent upon a somatosensory-based awareness of the body (a body scheme) that is derived from sensory feedback from previous movement. Body scheme is the inner awareness of body parts, how they fit together, and how they move through space. As we move, we are constantly generating proprioceptive and tactile input (called feedback) from our actions. That proprioceptive feedback becomes the foundation for later actions that we engage in (called feedforward). For example, we have all walked up many stairways and are completely unaware of how high a step is. It is only if the step is too high or too low that we

This child is creatively exploring a box, illustrating all three steps of praxis.

become aware of it. The body scheme is constantly integrating new sensory experiences on which we can base new motor activities.

For the most part the body scheme, and the motor planning based on it, is automatic and subconscious. For children with motor planning deficits, many learned motor activities, such as stair climbing, are effortful and require concentration. It is as if these children are doing a motor task for the first time each time they perform it—the task never becomes automatic. Motor planning also involves the ability to sequence motor tasks into projected action sequences (Koomar & Bundy, 1991)—for example, climbing to the top of a slide, sitting down while holding onto the edge of the slide, and finally sliding down to the bottom while squealing in delight. The final step of praxis is **execution**—actually doing the activity. Successful execution requires coordination and motor skill, as well as adequate ideation and motor planning.

Dyspraxia refers to problems in conceptualizing,

organizing, and directing unfamiliar purposeful action. (Dyspraxia is not the same as apraxia, a term that refers to the inability of people who have suffered a stroke or other brain damage to articulate speech or perform actions that were once familiar). Children who have dyspraxia have problems in either ideation or motor planning. They often also have problems in execution that can contribute to their performance deficit. In typically developing young children, flexibility and creativity are the hallmark of their praxis, or approach to new situations. Thus, absence of flexibility and creativity are the strongest indicators of dyspraxia. There are no specific developmental schedules of praxis. In a given activity, one child may exhibit praxis; another child of the same age may not. Praxis emerges from the interaction between the environment and the child. One cannot underestimate the pervasiveness of praxis during the early childhood years. We passed a child recently in the hallway and glibly asked, "What's new?" He stopped, reflected, and said, "Everything." Very young children are continuously confronted with new and complex demands that must be negotiated using praxis skills.

Observations of two young children in a playgroup illustrate praxis. Billy was an active 2 1/2-year-old toddler who demonstrated excellent praxis. He was inventive in planning and sequencing novel motor acts during his play. Billy enthusiastically claimed one of the big dump trucks as he entered the room. He began by propelling the truck around the edge of the play space, making lots of truck sounds and loading his truck with smaller trucks, balls, and animals. Once the truck was full, he roared to the city dump (his mother's lap) and unloaded his treasures. After a few minutes of this activity. he proceeded to build a road out of large blocks and raced his vehicles with glee in his make-believe speedway. Billy then pretended that each vehicle carried a circus animal as he had seen on television. The parade started with an elephant and ended with a camel. Eventually, Billy pushed the cars and trucks down the pretend sidewalk at crashing speeds. In contrast to Billy's flexible and creative play, James was much less active. James, also a 2 1/2-year-old, had dyspraxia. He found little to do with his vehicles. He watched Billy's elaborate play but did not join him. Instead he pushed his trucks back and forth in a straight path, spun the wheels with his finger, and lined them up in an orderly row. He did try to "drive" his truck on Billy's road, but he had difficulty keeping his truck on the road and kept tripping on and misplacing the blocks. Within a short time, he became distracted and decided just to watch Billy and the other children. James did not have the ideation or motor planning necessary to keep up with the changing, active play of the other toddlers—he was more comfortable with his familiar activities.

Diagnostic classification of sensory-related mental health and developmental disorders of infants and toddlers

In this chapter, we have described sensory modulation profiles as one way of categorizing children's sensory functioning. Sensory profiles expressed in terms of the "four A's" are particularly useful in distinguishing between children whose sensory-related behaviors may appear similar but stem from different underlying problems in sensory processing. We have also introduced the terms praxis and dyspraxia, which help us to focus attention on the problems of children who have difficulty using sensory input to act flexibly and creatively in producing novel motor acts. Both sensory modulation profiles and the concept of dyspraxia are based on the underlying capacity to process sensory input. The sensory profile is a descriptive framework that provides insight into the underlying sensory or motor dysfunction that underlies and contributes to worrisome behavior. In contrast, ZERO TO THREE's *Diagnostic Classification of Mental Health and Developmental Disorders of Infancy and Early Childhood (DC:0-3)* (1994) focuses primarily on very young children's affective, behavioral, and relational functioning. However, *DC:0-3*, unlike systems of mental health classification developed for older children and adults, recognizes the critical role that sensory processing plays in the overall behavior and development of infants and toddlers. The system describes two major diagnostic categories that reflect problems in sensory integration—regulatory disorders and multisystem developmental disorders (disorders of relating and communicating).

Regulatory Disorders

According to *DC:0-3*, a diagnosis of regulatory disorder in an infant or young child requires both a distinct behavioral pattern and a related sensory, sensorimotor, or organizational processing difficulty. The processing deficit interferes with the child's ability to manage a calm, alert, or emotionally positive state. There are underlying physiological, sensory, attentional, motor, or affective processes that disrupt behavioral regulation. The following are common symptoms of regulatory disorders:

• under or over-reactivity to sensory stimuli (e.g., touch, lights, sounds, odors, temperature, movement);

• poor sleeping and eating patterns;

• deficits in motor planning;

• dysfunction in auditory processing;

• problems in fine motor control;

• poor visual-spatial processing;

• limited attentional skills; and

• deficits in the range and depth of emotional expression.

DC:0-3 identifies four types of regulatory disorders that couple a sensory processing deficit with a behavioral pattern: hypersensitive, under-reactive, motorically disorganized and impulsive, and "other." These are general categories that are not mutually exclusive. A child may have symptoms from a number of categories, may fit across a combination of the types, or may not fit into any one predominant pattern (Lieberman, Wieder, & Fenichel, 1997).

1. Young children who are over-reactive to sensory stimuli are termed **hypersensitive**. A child's level of hypersensitivity is often inconsistent and variable, based on such factors as the time of day, previous sensory experience, and fatigue. Two behavioral patterns are characteristic of the hypersensitive type of regulatory disorder—fearful and cautious, and negative and defiant.

• **Fearful and cautious**. These children are often on sensory overload and feel that they could "'jump out of their skin." They are frequently frightened, anxious and worried that the sights, sounds, and movements around them will be overpowering. Therefore, these children tend to be hypervigilant, avoid transitions, and prefer routine.

• **Negative and defiant**. When young, these children are fussy, difficult, and resistant to change. When older, they are frequently negative, angry, and stubborn, with a tendency to be compulsive and perfectionistic. Children with a negative and defiant behavioral pattern are often tactile-defensive, over-reactive to sound, and demonstrate poor auditory processing. Problems in fine motor coordination and motor planning are also common.

2. Children who are hyposensitive to sensory stimuli are classified as **under-reactive**. They are divided into two categories—withdrawn and difficult to engage, and self-absorbed.

• **Withdrawn and difficult to engage.** Hyporeactivity is often noted to sound and movement in space. Tactile responsivity is variable. Auditory-verbal processing is usually deficient as well as motor planning. At times, these children seek out repetitive vestibular activity such as spinning and swinging. They typically appear lethargic, apathetic, and easily exhausted. They do not have the sensory support that fuels them for engagement and exploration. Instead these children appear unresponsive to social contact and sensation and may seem to be depressed.

• **Self-absorbed.** These children are preoccupied by their sensations, thoughts, and emotions. They may also be distractible and inattentive. They often escape into fantasies that are creative and full of imagination. This pattern of tuning out the world and focusing on one's inner life is frequently associated with receptive language difficulties. Problems in sensory or motor processing may be present, but not always.

3. The third type of regulatory disorder is labeled **motorically disorganized and impulsive**. These are generally children with poor motor planning, under-reactivity to sensory input (particularly touch and sound), and high activity level. They seek out sensory-rich experiences that provide somatosensory stimulation. This often leads to aggressive, impulsive behavior characteristic of risk-taking. They lack caution and are often fearless. The overall excitability and disorganization of behavior may cause these children to be motorically unfocused, inattentive, and occasionally destructive. Auditory or visual-spatial processing deficits may be present.

4. The fourth type of regulatory problem is termed simply "**other,**" since children in this category do not have a definable or consistent behavioral pattern. They have deficits in sensory or motor processing, but their behaviors do not fit into any of the previously described types of regulatory disorders.

As we have noted, the *DC:0-3* diagnostic category of regulatory disorders is both similar to and different from the sensory modulation profiles we have described in this monograph. Probably the major difference is what is at the core of each classification system. Our profiles are based on the sensory functioning of children—the underlying capacity to process sensory input. We have tried to maintain a consistency in the sensory-based aspects of the profiles since our intervention (as discussed in Chapter 5) begins with that understanding. The *DC:0-3* taxonomy, in contrast, focuses on the behavioral or personality characteristics of children with regulatory disorders. For example, both systems recognize the linear relationship between the hyperreactive/hypersensitive child and the hyporeactive/under-reactive child. However, in the demarcation of subtypes, children who are described as "fearful and cautious" in the *DC:0-3* system could be hyper- or hyporeactive in the taxonomy based solely on the sensory profile. Likewise, a child who fits the "withdrawn and difficult to engage" *DC:0-3* subtype could be either a child who is truly hyporeactive or a hyperreactive child who is in physiological shutdown. Similarly, the "'motorically disorganized and impulsive" child described in *DC:0-3* typically has motor planning problems which are part of our description of dyspraxia. But it is also possible that the motorically disorganized child is not dyspraxic at all but is taking risks in order to engage in sensory seeking to achieve optimal arousal.

Each classification system contributes to our understanding of children with problems in self-regulation. They both recognize the interface between sensory processing and behavioral expression. However, they emphasize different aspects of the condition. It is helpful for the reader to keep both systems in mind as we move to discussions of assessment and intervention in Chapters 4 and 5.

Multisystem Developmental Disorder

Like Regulatory Disorders, the diagnostic category of Multisystem Developmental Disorder (M S D D) is a new contribution of the *DC:0-3* system. Many clinicians who work with children under three years of age who have severe disorders of relating and communicating find that the diagnoses of Pervasive Developmental Disorder - Not Otherwise Specified and Autism Spectrum Disorders are rigid and confining. These diagnoses suggest to some that

A father uses vestibular
input to engage his son.

children with these disorders have little or no capacity for
engagement. In reality, many young children whose behavior has autistic features encompass a range of ability to
establish relationships, regulate affective expression, and
process sensory and cognitive information. The issue is
whether these children with "mixed features" should be
categorized in the autism spectrum.

DC:0-3 includes a classification of Multisystem
Developmental Disorder for these children with a mixed
presentation. It suggests that their primary deficit is not
relating per se, but the motor and sensory processing
problems that interfere with the organization of sensory
input and affect necessary for social relatedness. The diagnosis of M S D D is appropriate for children who have a
significant impairment in communication and sensorimotor processing, but exhibit some capacity for interpersonal relatedness. Children diagnosed with M S D D have a

Many children are overstimulated and unregulated during holidays.

disability that is more severe than those who meet the diagnostic criteria for *DC:0-3*'s regulatory disorder classification. They evidence:

• a major deficit in the ability to engage in social-emotional relations with a primary caregiver;

• a significant impairment in communication;

• dysfunction in auditory processing; and

• impairments in general sensory processing.

The sensory and motor deficits of these children are particularly germane to this discussion. Although they function at a range of developmental levels, many of these children are hyper- or hyposensitive to sensory input. Many have a mixed presentation: Most typically, they are over-reactive to tactile and auditory input and under-reactive to vestibular and proprioceptive sensation. As a result, they often crave stimulation that involves spinning, twirling, and sensory-based activities such as opening and closing doors. Muscle tone is often low, and ideation, motor planning, and awareness of position in space are limited. Children with M S D D typically resist change and tend to perseverate in a preoccupied fashion with a few favorite objects, such as toy trucks or cars.

The inclusion of Regulatory Disorder and Multisystem Developmental Disorder in the DC:0-3 system of diagnostic classification is noteworthy for several reasons. First, it represents a recognition among leaders in the field of infant mental health that sensory integration directly influences the behavior of young children. Second, the descriptions of these categories in DC: 0-3 and related case studies (Lieberman, Wieder & Fenichel, 1997) vividly illustrate how difficulties in sensory integrative deficits can interfere with the infant's moment-to-moment living and psychological development. Third, these conceptualizations suggest that children's problems in relating and communicating may be secondary to the more primary deficiencies of sensory integration. These deficits must be addressed in order to free the child to acquire higher-order communicative, cognitive, and social-emotional skills.

Summary

Sensory modulation is the ability to manage one's reaction to sensation and is reflected by the child's sensory threshold. Disorders in modulation are described in the following profiles: hyperreactivity, sensory avoidant, hyporeactivity, and sensory seeking. Another type of sensory integrative disorder is dyspraxia, which is a problem in using sensory input to produce unfamiliar purposeful action. Building upon this discussion, we now turn to important issues related to assessment.

CHAPTER 4

Assessment

Individual differences in sensory processing do not inevitably lead to difficulties in development or learning. This is important to remember as we consider screening and assessment of sensory integration. Greater understanding of sensory integration and self-regulation can equip all parents and caregivers to help infants and young children interact more successfully with the environment. When children are having difficulty in self-regulation, the process of screening and assessment of sensory modulation and praxis can lead the way to meaningful intervention.

The key to both screening and assessment of sensory integration is to focus on *how* a child processes sensory information and manages environmental challenges. Because sensory integration is about the *process* through which a child organizes sensory experience for use, tests or procedures that simply measure whether or not a child can demonstrate mastery of specific skills will not tell us whether a child might benefit from intervention. Instead, assessment involves systematic observation of three different contributors to sensory integrative function—the child, the physical environment, and the social environment—and the dynamic goodness-of-fit among them. One must assess the situational demands, the sensory properties of the physical and social environments, and the resources and capacities that the child brings to interactions in order to understand the goodness-of-fit between the child and the environment. This kind of assessment requires thoughtful observation of the child in different situations over time. Moreover, assessment does not occur only when a child is initially referred for evaluation. The assessment process must be an integral part of the planning and execution of sensory integrative intervention. The clinician must continuously assess the child's behavior in order to grade and modify intervention based

> Assessment involves systematic observation of the child, the physical environment, and the social environment.

upon the child's changing abilities, responses, and intrinsic motivation.

This chapter first presents general guidelines for screening and assessment of sensory integration. It then addresses ways of gathering information over time through: 1) qualitative observation of the child and the context (i.e., the physical and social environments), 2) parent interview and questionnaires, and 3) standardized instruments. Lastly, we discuss interpretation of assessment data which leads to intervention planning.

General guidelines for screening and assessment of sensory integration

A *screening* provides an overall measure of the child's functioning in a particular domain and identifies whether there is a need for further assessment. A professional who is knowledgeable about child development from any of a variety of disciplinary perspectives is capable of conducting a screening. However, assessment of a child's functioning in a particular area of concern should be conducted by a professional with specialized training in that domain. Thus a well-trained primary health care provider, early care and education professional, or early intervention provider could screen a child to determine whether he or she is having problems in motor control and sensory modulation, but an occupational therapist would be the most appropriate professional to complete a comprehensive assessment of sensory integration.

The following guidelines establish important parameters for performing quality screening and assessment of sensory integration.

• **Focus on** *how* **the child processes sensory information and manages environmental challenges**—not solely on the specific skills the child displays or developmental milestones he or she has achieved. This approach entails a dynamic *process* orientation to assessment in addition to the *product* focus typical of most developmental evaluations (Coster, 1998; Greenspan & Meisels, 1996). For instance, we are interested in the fact that a child has achieved the developmental milestone of being able to build a 7-block-high tower. But we are also interested in analyzing the child's attention, task persistence, grasp patterns, problem solving, and other qualitative aspects of

Much can be learned from observing unstruc-tured peer play.

performance. Likewise, we complement our observation of a child's repetitive rocking by investigating what environmental conditions precede or follow this behavior. Such qualitative information enables the practitioner to understand the child and design meaningful intervention when necessary.

• **Use interviews with parents and observation of the child in natural situations** as your primary methods of gathering information about a child's capacity to process sensory information in the context of relationships, play, and functional activities (Dunn, Brown, & McGuigan, 1994). It is especially helpful to talk with parents about their experiences and to observe the child directly in the following situations:

- independent and social free play;
- meal times, bathing and other functional activities;
- structured and unstructured peer interaction;
- parent-child interaction; and
- transitions between activities.

• **Look at the relationship between the child and environmental challenges** (Hanft & Place, 1996). Do not look at the child in isolation during the assessment process, and avoid focusing on "pathology." Remember that functional difficulties can arise from a poor fit between the child's sensory needs, available resources for self-regulation, and environmental demands. For example, a child who is dis-

The mother is whispering to her baby in an intimate space to help modulate arousal.

tractible during play may be responding not to internally driven impulsivity but to the over-stimulating lights, sounds, and activities in a busy playroom. In this example, the primary difficulty is found in the environment and not within the child. The poor fit between child and environment creates the difficulty (distractibility) which may compromise development and learning.

• **Remember that the response to sensation builds up over time and is cumulative.** We must keep this phenomenon in mind during assessment as well as intervention. One child may be more sensitive to touch at the end of a long day than in the morning. Another may be slow to register input because of a high threshold but can rapidly become overloaded by accumulated sensation. The influence of sensory input is not always immediately observable. In assessment, we are looking for connections between the child's behavior and previous, as well as current, sensory experiences. The assessor must take care that any changes in the amount or type of sensory input provided to the child be made slowly and conservatively.

• **Monitor the child's level of arousal, since it influences responsivity**. If the child is highly aroused, it is likely that he or she will respond to the surroundings in a hypersensitive or disorganized manner. In contrast, if the child is under-aroused, there is a tendency to respond in a sluggish, hyposensitive fashion. In screening and assessment, therefore, one must determine the child's current arousal level as a baseline for interpreting behavior. The examiner needs to assess whether or not the present level of arousal is typical of the child's functioning or not. Extremes in arousal will bias the examiner's observations and findings.

• **Include repeated observations over time in any assessment of sensory integration.** All babies and toddlers vary in their behavior from day to day, and children with sensory processing problems are more variable than predictable in their performance. At any given time, the consistency of a child's behavior can be influenced by: 1) the degree of environmental stimulation; 2) the child's current emotional state, general level of arousal, coping skills, and resources; 3) accumulated sensory build-up; and 4) the availability of a familiar caregiver.

• **Identify the possible sensory basis for stereotypic and repetitive behaviors and the functions they serve for the child.** Stereotypic and repetitive sensory-based behaviors may serve different functions, depending on the child's current sensory threshold (Anzalone & Williamson, 2000; Baranek, 1999; Baranek, Foster, & Berkson, 1997a, 1997b). A child who is hyperreactive at a given moment (i.e., with a low threshold for sensory input) may use hand-flapping to gain selective focus and to screen out the rest of the visual environment. The outcome can be calming and organizing. The child who is hyporeactive (i.e., with a high threshold for sensory input) may use this same behavior to increase arousal and activation. A third child may use hand-flapping to discharge tension. Practitioners must use their knowledge of sensory processing to understand these stereotypical mannerisms and rituals.

Observing mother and son in a natural play situation.

• **Provide the opportunity for choice, self-initiation, creativity, and flexible problem solving during the assessment process.** Do not over-structure the assessment environment. During part of the time, the examiner and parents need to step back and avoid controlling the environmental conditions or initiating interactions. Directiveness on the part of the examiner, while necessary for certain types of testing, can restrict the expression of individual differences during qualitative observation. Planning for some unstructured time during the assessment period is especially important to observe praxis—a child's ability to conceptualize, organize, and carry out unfamiliar actions.

• Remember that assessment of sensory integration is only part of the information necessary to understand sensory processing. Perceptual discrimination is based upon the child's sensory modulation and higher order cognitive processes. The primary perceptual functions to be assessed in young children include visual, auditory, and tactile discrimination. Sample higher order perceptual skills include visual or auditory figure-ground perception, visuospatial relations, auditory memory, tactile localization, and stereognosis. Assessment of these functions is beyond the scope of this chapter, but it is discussed elsewhere in the clinical literature (e.g., Lezak, 1995; Schneck, 1996; Wetherby & Prizant, in press).

Qualitative observation

Observation is our most reliable tool for identifying problems and planning intervention for children who have difficulties in sensory integration. Standardized instruments do not reliably capture individual differences in this aspect of performance, since it is so variable and dependent upon each child's prior experiences. To learn the most we can about a child's capacity for sensory integration, we must pay attention to both the *child* and the *context* as we observe. It is helpful to compare the child's behavior in structured and unstructured circumstances. Structured situations include formal evaluations and adult-controlled situations. Unstructured situations may include individual free play, gross motor exploration, and activities of daily living. The practitioner should observe the child's performance in relation to the sensory demands of the environment (e.g., a child's increased arousal and impulsivity would be interpreted differently in a disorganized versus a quiet setting) as well as the cognitive, attentional, or motoric demands of the task.

Observation of the child

The practitioner observes the child's reactivity during engagement in a variety of tasks as well as the child's global behavioral organization in terms of the "four A's." Observation focuses on the influence of sensory input and its impact on the child's self-regulation of arousal, attention, affect, and action. Since the child's reactivity to sensory input is cumulative, we observe the child's behavior on multiple occasions over time. For example, we can draw few if any conclusions from our observation of the temper tantrum that a toddler exhibits in our office in the late morning after three hours in a busy child care center and a car trip with anxious parents. We need to find out from parents whether this is the way the child typically responds to sensory buildup and when and where we can observe the child's feeling more comfortable and organized. In other words, we must *expect* young children with sensory processing difficulties to vary their performance. Variability, then, is not an indicator of unreliability in the assessment protocol but, rather, a real phenomenon that should be looked for during the assessment process. Our challenge as an evaluator is to record the range of a child's responses and the sensory conditions that support optimal performance as well as the types of conditions that are problematic.

The following list of questions focuses observation on sensory-based behavioral organization in the child. The list is categorized according to the "four A's." The questions provide a structure for the examiner during screening and assessment.

Arousal

- What is the child's state of alertness, and how does it change in response to different sensory experiences?

- Is the child able to transition smoothly between different states of alertness?

- Is the child able to sustain levels of energy and activity that support successful task engagement?

- Does the child have a narrow or wide range of optimal arousal?

- Does the child have a range of coping strategies that enable the child to modulate sensory reactivity and arousal?

Attention

- Is the child able to maintain selective focus on relevant stimuli?

- Is the child able to shift attention between two or more targets or sensory modalities?

- Is the duration of the child's attention span comparable to that of other children of the same age?

- When attending to tasks, does the child seem to be using more effort than other children of the same age?

• Does the child appear to be hypervigilant or non-responsive to sensory-based activities?

• Is the child able to independently select a focus for attention, or is he or she dependent upon adults to structure the environment to support attention?

• Does the child prefer or avoid certain sensory modalities?

Affect

• Does the child have an organized and complete range of emotional expression?

• What is the relationship between the child's emotional expression and sensation?

• Is there a predominant emotional tone characteristic of the child (e.g., fearfulness, anxiety, defiance, flatness, or withdrawal)?

• Is the child available for social interaction with peers and/or adults?

• Does the child have a playful disposition that reflects ease in the situation and supports learning and engagement?

Action

• Is the child able to formulate goals for play behavior that are appropriate to his or her developmental skills and environmental opportunities?

• Is the child able to solve problems encountered during exploration or play with creativity, flexibility, and persistence?

• Does the child avoid or seem unduly stressed by novel objects or environments?

• Does the child consistently engage in the same activities regardless of environmental affordances?

• Is the child able to successfully complete activities once undertaken?

• Is the child able to transition easily between different activities or settings?

• Is the child's behavior characterized by consistent approach or avoidance of specific materials or tasks?

• Does the child seem unaware of the body, with frequent tripping, bumping into things, or accidents?

• Does the child have adequate motor planning and coordination for age-appropriate tasks?

When observations of a child suggest that he or she is having difficulty with action, a practitioner should consider the possibility of dyspraxia. A child may have difficulty with one or a combination of the three components of praxis—ideation, motor planning, and execution. These difficulties are best observed in unstructured situations, especially play. Since children with dyspraxia often rely on familiar, "over-learned" behavior and activities, any observation of praxis must provide unexpected, novel situations that challenge the child's ability to respond flexibly, choose a goal, and solve a problem using motor skills. Observation focuses on *how* the child plans and sequences his or her approach to these new situations.

Diagnosis of a disorder of praxis is difficult. Concerned practitioners and parents who have the opportunity to observe a child in many situations over time should screen for the following behaviors indicative of children with dyspraxia:

• inflexibility—the child perseverates on one aspect of a task and has difficulty in making transitions;

• lack of sensorimotor exploration—the child may be unable to climb onto a structure to get an appealing toy;

• limited complexity of play—the child may be inactive or simply line up or spin toys;

• restricted problem-solving of new tasks;

• behavioral rigidity;

• low frustration tolerance;

• presence of "crash" solutions to terminate demanding activities—the child may knock down or throw toys to get out of a task or situation;

• lack of organization in performance of activities;

• slow and visually directed performance;

• clothes in disarray and/or unfastened;

• poor quality of fine motor skills;

• poor temporal awareness and sequencing of daily living tasks—the child puts his shirt on backwards or before taking his pajamas off;

• avoidance of group activities and peer play;

• preference for adult one-to-one interaction; and

• excessive concern with adult appraisal of performance.

If screening indicates a possible problem in praxis, a trained occupational therapist should observe the child in numerous settings under diverse conditions to determine the nature of the problem. Is the breakdown in task engagement due to a sensorimotor deficit or some other factor such as distractibility or impulsivity? Is this a sensory processing/praxis deficit or primarily an issue of motor strength and coordination? Is the difficulty due to ideation, motor planning, and/or execution? Limited **ideation** means that a child is unable to formulate new goals specific to situational demands; the child has no idea what to do, or is rigid and inflexible in forming goals. A child who has a deficit in **motor planning** knows what he or she wants to do (for example, climb onto a structure) but cannot organize movement patterns to achieve the goal. The major means of assessing praxis is through observation of the child's approach to novel gross and fine-motor tasks. The assessor needs to provide a range of opportunities for the child to engage in activities that require the control of large muscles as well as fine manipulation—for example, objects to climb over or under, an unusual swing, or a new manipulative toy that is perched on top of a climbing structure.

Observation of the context

It is the interaction between the child and the environment that produces sensory-related behavior. Therefore, to understand the sensory processing of the child, we must observe the context in which the child is functioning. The practitioner should observe the child and the context *simultaneously*, in order to determine the goodness-of-fit between the two elements (Schaaf & Anzalone, in press; Zeitlin & Williamson, 1994). Without an understanding of this connection the practitioner can make incorrect clinical assumptions. For example, a child may demonstrate defensive behaviors such as gagging, spitting up, and facial grimacing during feedings. These behaviors could be interpreted as hypersensitivity in the oral area. However, by paying attention to the environmental context, the practitioner may realize that the caregiver is feeding the child too quickly. The child's aversive reaction is not sensory-based but, rather, an indication of an inappropriate feeding technique.

The examiner needs to appreciate the sensory attributes of the environment and how well they match the child's capacity for self-regulation and organization. The following questions can help to focus observation on critical aspects of the physical and social environments.

• What sensory input is characteristic of the physical and social environments (e.g., visual, auditory, tactile, proprioceptive, vestibular)?

• What are the sensory properties of the identified sensory systems (e.g., location, intensity, and duration)?

• Does the environment require the child to organize information simultaneously from different sensory systems for a response?

• What is the quality of the physical environment in terms of temperature, lighting, noise, space, and related properties?

• What are the social characteristics of the situation (e.g., adult or peer, individualized or group, verbal or nonverbal, child- or adult-directed)?

• What are the specific environments, situations, or individuals that are particularly organizing for the child?

• What are the specific environments, situations, or individuals that are particularly challenging or disorganizing for the child?

• Does the environment provide a routine that is reasonably predictable, consistent, and structured?

• Does the environment allow (or require) flexible and creative interaction?

The physical environment in Figure 4.1 is chaotic and overcrowded. Since the children are sensorially assaulted, most become detached and distracted. In contrast, the quiet space in another child care center has features that promote self-regulation (see Figure 4.2). The children learn to go to this area when they need to "cool down and chill out."

The practitioner's observation of the social context and interpretation of the sensory and affective contributions to the parent-child relationship can provide the foundation for meaningful intervention. In assessing the social environment, the practitioner should be particularly concerned with the nature of the child's interactions with parents, other caregivers, and peers. Mutual attention, connection, and communication are sophisticated achieve-

A chaotic overcrowded environment that may lead to sensory overload.

This organized space in a a child care center promotes self-regulation.

ments that do not occur automatically. For example, some fussy, sensorially disorganized babies are irritable and cry excessively during their early months. The parents often attend to them diligently for weeks on end without sleep or satisfaction. In some cases, this exhausting scenario leads to an unhappy outcome—by the time the infant becomes stable and organized, the parent has emotionally disengaged. On the other hand, a parent, caregiver, sibling, or playmate may have discovered—or been helped to learn—strategies that help a baby or young child regulate attention, arousal and affect, and organize behavior. During an assessment, the practitioner should watch carefully for the kinds of interactions that support a child's best performance.

Parent interview and questionnaires

Parents and other significant caregivers can provide important information regarding the child's ability to modulate sensory input in a variety of situations. Semi-structured interviews and standardized questionnaires are particularly useful in talking with parents and caregivers about a child's sensory processing and regulation because they frame the child's behavior in a new way—often a valuable intervention in itself.

The sensory diet

Questions about a child's "sensory diet" (Wilbarger, 1995; Williams and Shellenberger, 1996) allow the practitioner to construct a profile of naturally occurring activities throughout the day that provide sensory input and influence the child's regulation of the "four A's." The profile provides data about the child's sensory tolerances and preferences as they are reflected in daily activity and the behavioral regulation of arousal, attention, affect, and action. It also identifies periods of behavioral organization and disorganization during the day and relates that organization to ongoing sensory experiences and environmental demands. Some situations that provide valuable insight into sensory integration are playtime, mealtimes, bathing, diapering, disruptions in typical routines, and preferences in clothing or play.

The following questions may generate a productive conversation with the parent or caregiver regarding a child's sensory processing and how it influences child and family functioning. These questions are designed to provide a starting point for a discussion which is then followed up with skillful probing using semi-structured interview techniques. They should be used selectively, based on the presenting needs of the child and family.

• What is your child's typical day like?

• What types of sensory activities does your child like and dislike?

• How does your child manage transitions and changes in daily routines?

• Is there a predictable time of day or type of activity when your child is most and/or least organized?

• Are your child's activities of daily living and self-care tasks limited by sensory or motor problems (e.g., does not tolerate textured foods, fearful during bathing, strong clothing preferences)?

• Does your child have habits and routines that support daily functioning?

• How does your child respond to affectionate physical touch or handling?

• Does your child initiate exploration of novel as well as familiar situations?

• Does your child enjoy playing with other children?

Standardized questionnaires

Semi-structured interviews can be supplemented by standardized questionnaires regarding the child's sensory and self-regulatory performance.

• The *Infant Toddler Symptom Checklist* (DeGangi & Poisson, 1995) addresses such areas as self-regulation, attention, sleeping, eating, dressing, bathing, movement, language, vision, and emotional functioning in children between 7 and 30 months of age.

• The *Sensorimotor History Questionnaire for Preschoolers* (DeGangi & Balzer-Martin, 1999) is a 51-item questionnaire that has been validated as a screening tool for 3- to 4-year-olds. It categorizes behavior in terms of self-regulation, sensory processing of touch, sensory processing of movement, emotional maturity, and motor maturity.

• The *Sensory Profile* (Dunn, 1999) is a parent questionnaire appropriate for assessing sensory processing of children between 3 and 10 years of age. Its 125 items address different sensory systems, activity level, movement, and emotional-social functioning. This questionnaire has been extensively studied with normative and clinical populations (Dunn & Brown, 1997; Dunn & Westman, 1997; Kientz & Dunn, 1997).

• The *Short Sensory Profile* (McIntosh, Miller, Shyu, & Dunn, 1999) is an abbreviated version of the *Sensory Profile* with sound psychometric properties. The *Short Sensory Profile* has 38 items in 7 subscales: tactile sensitivity, taste/smell sensitivity, under-responsive/seeks sensation, auditory filtering, visual/auditory sensitivity, low energy/weak, and movement sensitivity.

• The *Functional Behavior Assessment for Children With Sensory Integrative Dysfunction* (Cook, 1991) provides a way to gather data regarding sensory-related activities of daily living through parent interview.

• The *Sensory Integration Observation Guide for Children From Birth to Three* (Jirgal & Bouma, 1989) is presented in Table 4.1. This questionnaire provides a useful age-related guideline for interviewing parents and observing children. A version of this guide modified for children from 0 to 12 months of age is available online from www.sinetwork.org.

Table 4.1

Sensory Integration Observation Guide

Tirgal and Bouma, 1989. Reprinted with permission of the American Occupational Therapy Association.

Level 1 (approximately birth to 12 months of age)

1. Does the baby like to be held and tend to mold the body to that of adult holding him or her? (Conversely, does the baby show arching behavior or attempt to pull or push away when held?)

2. Is the baby comfortable being moved? (Conversely, does the baby become irritable or disorganized when passively moved in space or when the body position is changed?)

3. Does the baby have favorite songs and movement games with adults and anticipate these special interactions?(Conversely, does the baby avoid any novel play situations?)

4. Does the baby explore toys orally at the appropriate age? (Conversely, does the baby avoid mouthing toys?)

5. Does the baby accept textured foods when they are introduced at the appropriate age? (Conversely, does the baby have difficulty handling textured foods, or is he or she a very picky eater?)

6. Can the baby attend to more than one stimulus at one time (e.g., look and listen at the same time)? (Conversely, does the baby "tune out" if more than one stimulus is presented at one time?)

7. At an appropriate age and motor ability level, does the baby easily move from one position to another in play? (Conversely, does the baby prefer to stay in one position and avoid transitional movements?)

8. Were the baby's sleep-wake cycles fairly well-established after the first 6 weeks? (Conversely, has the baby never developed an established pattern of routines, or is the baby difficult to calm or get to sleep?)

9. Does the baby engage in a variety of progressive midline play—two hands together, transfer, and crossing the midline? (Conversely, does the baby use one hand or the other but avoid bilateral use?)

10. Does the baby show a preference for certain sensory stimuli (e.g., music or touch)? (Conversely, do caregivers have difficulty determining the baby's preference for any sensory input?)

11. Does the baby show an appropriate response to sensory-induced reflexes (e.g., rooting, protective extension, or righting responses?)

Level 2 (approximately 12-18 months of age)

1. Does the child enjoy exploring a variety of new textures? Will the child play with foods, textured toys, and so on? (Conversely, does the child avoid finger feeding or withdraw from touching new textures, even an attractive toy?)

2. Does the child's toy play progress from one level to the next in an easy flow – that is, does the child combine toys at an appropriate age? (Conversely, does the child's play seem "stuck" at an

immature level, such as mouthing, banging, or casting in a repetitive fashion?)

3. Does the child spend time exploring a toy to obtain information about all of its components parts? Does the child use touch, vision, and hearing together to assess properties of toys such as squeak toys or balls in a bowl? (Conversely, does the child show poor exploration of the component parts or details of toys? Does the child have a short attention span when given a new toy?)

4. Is the child able to follow simple directions with and without gestures? Does the child seem to be listening and looking when an adult talks to him or her? (Conversely, does the child show inconsistent responses to verbal directions and make poor eye contact when an adult talks to him or her?)

5. Does the child accept having different textures of clothing next to the skin, or is he or she more comfortable with less clothing on (e.g., no shoes or short shirts)? (Conversely, is the child very fussy about clothing? Does the child not like to be barefooted?

Level 3 (approximately 18 months to 3 years of age)

1. Does the child seem to modulate his or her activity level appropriately to given play situations (e.g., active versus passive play or structured play)? (Conversely, does the child have an excessive need for intense movement or proprioception, such as jumping, rocking and swinging, or does the child avoid movement altogether?)

2. Does the child explore new play equipment with anticipation and show good motor planning and balance skills? (Conversely, does the child avoid novel play situations or show difficulty getting on and off age-appropriate play equipment? Is the child clumsy, or does he or she want to remain on the ground all the time?)

3. Does the child demonstrate an ability to remain focused on a task despite moderate levels of environmental visual and auditory activity? (Conversely, does the child seem to be auditory or visually distractible when playing with other children?)

4. Can the child participate well in group activities? Does the child seem to understand the sequence of and changes in activities? (Conversely, does the child seem lost when in group or circle activities?)

5. Is the child comfortable trying new things or with changes in plans? (Conversely, does the child become upset if routines or plans are changed?)

Standardized instruments

Relatively few standardized performance-based tools are available to assess sensory integration, including praxis. Table 4.2 lists commercially available standardized tools (both performance- based and parent interview) available to assess sensory integration.

• The *Test of Sensory Functions in Infants* (DeGangi & Greenspan, 1989) is a diagnostic, criterion-referenced test designed to be administered by professionals trained in child development and sensory processing. It is designed to assess infants and toddlers with regulatory disorders, developmental delay, and those at risk for learning disorders.

• The *Early Coping Inventory* (Zeitlin, Williamson, & Szczepanski, 1988) assesses the coping style of children 4 to 36 months of age. The coping behaviors of the children are observed over time in a variety of situations. This psychometrically sound tool is particularly sensitive in measuring sensory-based self-regulation and adaptation. It can be administered by any professional with a background in child development.

• *Sensory Integration and Praxis Tests* (Ayres, 1989) are a diagnostic, norm-referenced test battery designed for school-aged children who are relatively high-functioning. Sensory modulation is not directly measured on this instrument but can be inferred from qualitative observation. This battery has specific tests that measure different components of praxis (e.g., postural praxis, sequencing praxis, oral praxis, constructional praxis, or praxis on verbal command). This instrument requires extensive formal training and certification for reliable administration and is dependent on the child's having receptive language skills at least at the 4-year level. It is typically not used for children with autistic spectrum disorders or with significant developmental delay.

• *The Miller Assessment of Preschoolers* (Miller, 1988) is a norm-referenced test that provides a few items directly addressing a child's motor planning and can be used for screening for difficulties in praxis. Observation and clinical judgment by an appropriately trained practitioner are the most important factors in determining when praxis contributes to a performance deficit. The manual for this assessment provides many useful guidelines for observation.

Table 4.2
Assessment of Sensory Integration with Standardized Instruments

Name of test, Age range, Comments, Source

Early Coping Inventory
4-36 months

>The instrument addresses sensorimotor organization, reactivity, and self-initiation as the child copes with daily living.
>
>Zeitlin, S., Williamson, G.G., & Szczepanski, M. (1988), Scholastic Testing Service, 480 Meyer Road, Bensonville, IL 60106

Infant Toddler Symptom Checklist
7-30 months

>Parent questionnaire designed to elicit information on regulatory disorders and sensory processing in the context of functional activities.
>
>DeGangi, G.A., & Poisson, S. (1995). Therapy Skill Builders. 555 Academic Court, San Antonio, TX 78204

Miller Assessment of Preschoolers
2 years, 9 months-5 years, 8 months

>Developmental screening test that includes praxis items (imitation of postures and solving a maze).
>
>Miller, L.J. (1982). Psychological Corporation, 555 Academic Court, San Antonio, TX 78204

Sensory Integration and Praxis Tests
4.6-8.11 years

>12 subtests assess sensory and perceptual function in visual perceptual, visual, vestibular and postural, and somatosensory domains
>
>Ayres, A.J. (1989). Western Psychological Services, 12031 Wilshire Blvd., Los Angeles, CA 90025

The Sensory Profile
5-10 years (supplementary information of 3 & 4 year olds)

>Parent questionnaire with 125 items grouped into: sensory processing, modulation, and behavioral and emotional responses. Short Sensory Profile: a shorter version of this test (38 items) designed to target sensory modulation is also available.
>
>Dunn, W. (1999). Psychological Corporation, 555 Academic Court, San Antonio, TX 78204

Test of Sensory Functions in Infants
4-18 months

>Subtests include reactivity to tactile deep pressure and vestibular stimulation, adaptive motor functions, visual- tactile integration, and ocular-motor control.
>
>DeGangi, G.A. & Greenspan, S.I. (1989). Western Psychological Corporation, 12031 Wilshire Blvd., Los Angeles, CA 90025

Interpreting assessment data

To understand sensory integration, we must understand *how* a child engages in activities in his or her environment. Simply relating *what* a child is or is not able to do will not help us design meaningful interventions. Thus far we have described the importance of obtaining information about the child and environment through qualitative observation, interviews with parents, and standardized instruments. Once that information is obtained, the practitioner must synthesize data from these multiple sources in a theoretically sound way. This means going beyond reporting norm-referenced scores on assessment instruments or listing behaviors indicative of dysfunction. Similarly, it is not enough to know that a child is able to engage in exploratory play. The practitioner must also look at the conditions under which the child feels secure enough to explore, what types of materials the child investigates, which ones he or she refuses to approach, and the relevant sensory properties of each condition. The practitioner must observe relationships between the different sensory systems, behaviors, and the environment. Identifying these relationships is the first step in discerning critical themes or patterns of behavior.

The following questions illustrate the kind of clinical reasoning that underlies the process of interpreting findings from an assessment of sensory integration. Implicit in each question is the presenting functional problem that may have brought a child to the attention of an examiner and its potential sensory connections.

• Is there a sensory contribution to the child's presenting anxiety, as would occur in a child with sensory avoidance or hyperreactivity?

• Is there a sensory contribution to a strained parent-child attachment, as with Madeline and her limited ability to maintain self-regulation in the highly stimulating interactions offered by her mother?

• Is there a sensory contribution to the child's intolerance of certain types of clothing and or textured foods, characteristic of a hypersensitive child?

• Is there a relationship between a family's chaotic struggle to get ready for the day and the child's sensory defensiveness?

• Is there a pattern of sensory preferences or tolerances across sensory modalities, as exemplified by favored or avoided activities?

Table 4.3 presents a format for organizing assessment data in order to plan and implement intervention. This format helps the practitioner focus on the child's sensory processing, parental capacities and style, and the goodness-of-fit between the child and his or her physical and social environments. The practitioner examines possible areas for intervention and determines the extent to which each component of the overall profile promotes organization or disorganization in the child. Finally, this process helps the practitioner begin to plan intervention.

Interpreting assessment data presents many challenges to the clinician. As we observed at the beginning of this chapter, an understanding of sensory integration is most helpful as a way of understanding individual differences. Not all individual differences in sensory processing lead to functional consequences. For example, a baby who dislikes rough-and-tumble play may be offered many other ways to have fun by parents, siblings, and caregivers. A toddler who is slightly hypersensitive to vestibular input may avoid swings but be perfectly happy playing on other playground equipment. Similarly, no single behavior can be linked consistently to a single clinical profile or diagnostic category. Thus, the practitioner must use accumulated data concerning many behaviors, abilities, and situations in order to make a diagnostic decision or classification.

We must be cautious in interpreting the behavior and affect of children who may have sensory integrative deficits. For example, impulsive behavior may be seen in a child with hyperreactivity, sensory seeking, dyspraxia, or a regulatory disorder as described in *DC:0-3*. The underlying cause of the impulsivity is different in each case. The hyperreactive child acts impulsively to *escape* from an overwhelming stimulus, while the sensory-seeking child takes risks impulsively in order to get *more* sensation through his or her explorations. In contrast, the child with dyspraxia may simply appear to be impulsive because of clumsiness and poor motor planning.

A similar diagnostic challenge is present when a child appears flat and unavailable. In this situation, the practitioner should not assume that the child is hyporeactive. As previously mentioned, a child who appears unavailable

> An understanding of sensory integration is most helpful as a way of understanding individual differences.

Table 4.3

Organizing Assessment Data for Intervention

Component	Possible Issues for Intervention	Promotes organization or disorganization?	Intervention Implications
Child's state of nervous system and sensory modulation	• Hyperreactive • Sensory avoider • Hyporeactive • Sensory seeker • Mixed		
Parents	• Ability to read cues • Insight into child's difficulties • Synchrony or reciprocity • Ability to scaffold		
Goodness-of-Fit	• Social environment • Physical environment		
Child's self-regulation	• Arousal (including sleep/wake) • Activity level • Recovery or calming		
Child's specific sensory systems	• Tactile • Vestibular • Visual • Proprioceptive • Auditory • Olfactory • Temperature • Oral • Pain		
Child's sensory-based self-regulation	• Arousal • Attention • Affect • Action		

Modified from Schaaf & Anzalone (in press)

may actually be physiologically hyperreactive; the observable behavioral shutdown is the opposite of his internal state. In assessment, one must differentiate between these two profiles by grading the sensory experience. For example, systematically decreasing sensory input, providing organizing activity, and observing behavioral responses over time will differentiate between children in each profile. With decreased sensory input, the child who is truly hyperreactive will become calmer and more attentive, whereas the truly hyporeactive child may become more lethargic. It is also important to remember that not all sensory-seeking behaviors are associated with hyporeactivity. Some children with hyperreactivity or sensory defensiveness may engage in sensory seeking as a way of modulating their reactions to sensation (i.e., discharging tension or refocusing attention to organize themselves).

The observed behavior associated with various emotional responses may have roots in different underlying sensory-processing problems. Anxiety may be associated with hyperreactivity, sensory avoidance, or dyspraxia. Depression may be associated with hyporeactivity, sensory avoidance, or dyspraxia. Oppositional behavior may be linked to sensory avoidance or dyspraxia. Withdrawal may be associated with hyporeactivity, sensory avoidance, or dyspraxia. However, not all findings or behavioral problems have a sensory base. For instance, a child may not explore a toy because of limited motivation or lack of experience, rather than because of the sensory properties of the toy. Conversely, a child may ride on a swing for a long time "just because." The choice may not reflect any problems in sensory modulation of vestibular input. Emotions, such as anxiety or depression, may not have a sensory component for some children. Likewise, oppositional behavior could be related predominantly to psychosocial factors. To determine whether or not there is a sensory basis to a child's behavior, and whether that behavior is at all problematic, the practitioner uses skillful probing and structured observations.

Even when accumulated findings suggest strongly that a child's sensory differences are seriously compromising function, it is not always possible to understand the child's behavior in terms of an identifiable sensory profile such as those described in this document. A child may have a mixed and variable pattern of sensory processing that constitutes a unique clinical picture. The practitioner can then use the behavioral patterns described in the sensory modulation profiles for an initial understanding of the child, rather than as a rigid diagnostic categorization.

Summary

During the data collection stage of assessment, information is obtained about the child and environment through qualitative observation, parent interview, and standardized instruments. From data collection one moves to the interpretation stage of assessment, which provides a link to intervention planning. During this stage, integration and synthesis are emphasized and relationships between the different sensory systems, behaviors, and environments are explored. The interpretation stage ends with hypotheses about what, if any, sensory integrative abilities and deficits underlie the child's functioning. These findings and their implications are shared with the parents and other significant caregivers as the first step of intervention. Treatment continues at this point through the further refinement of hypotheses that guide intervention strategies. Assessment of sensory integration is ongoing and integrally involved in the intervention process.

CHAPTER 5

Intervention

Using a sensory integrative perspective to help young children interact more effectively with their environment involves three complementary strategies:

• helping parents and caregivers to understand sensory contributions to the child's behavior and to foster successful relationships between the child and significant others;

• modifying the environment to fit the child's needs; and

• providing individualized direct intervention designed to remediate identified problems.

Professionals who are knowledgeable about sensory processing and the components of a healthy sensory diet can implement the first two strategies. However, assessment and direct intervention by a specially trained occupational therapist is required for some children with difficulties in sensory-based self-regulation or praxis.

This chapter focuses first on ways to work collaboratively with parents. Next, it describes ways to grade the sensory experiences of children in natural environments. Finally, the clinical reasoning underlying direct intervention is discussed. Case studies of work with children who have hyperreactivity, hyporeactivity, and dyspraxia illustrate intervention strategies.

Collaborative work with parents

Effective intervention begins with helping the parent or caregiver to understand the child's specific sensory profile and how it relates to behavior (Holloway, 1998; Schaaf & Anzalone, in press; Wilbarger, 1995; Williams & Shellenberger, 1996). Understanding *why* a behavior occurs is the first step in responding sensitively to a child. A child's problems with sensory integration can make it very difficult for parents to interpret behavior and read his or her cues. Parents become more successful when they appreciate the sensory-based contributions to their child's behavior. This understanding is particularly relevant when sensory-related behaviors look the same as those that stem from a social or emotional source. For example, a baby with sensory defensiveness may arch away from a parent while being held. The parent may interpret this action as emotional rejection by the child rather than an expression of hypersensitivity to sensation. Another child may exhibit a flat, uninvested affect, which could be interpreted as a symptom of clinical depression although it might actually reflect either hyporeactivity or sensory avoidance. Aggressive behavior may also have a potential sensory foundation. A child who hits playmates may do so because of sensory defensiveness (i.e., he is protecting himself from incidental touch) rather than a psychological reason (i.e., she is fighting to dominate another child). Similarly, a child with sensory avoidance may demonstrate rigid controlling behavior as a strategy to create predictability in the environment, in order to diminish the likelihood of sensory overload. Of course, while it is essential to help parents and caregivers recognize sensory contributions to a child's behavior, it is equally important to avoid assuming that all behavior problems have a sensory basis.

Collaborative intervention with parents does not mean prescribing a "home program" but, rather, helping parents become sensitive observers of their child's sensory strengths and needs throughout the day. Practitioners need to help parents appreciate the extent to which naturally occurring activities and interactions within the child's daily routine provide the sensory input required to regulate or disrupt regulation of arousal, attention, affect, and action (the "four A's"). Intervention involves subtle modification of the child's sensory experiences during routines and activities. It also involves active problem solving on the part of caregivers to meet the child's needs in sensory modulation and praxis. Intervention does not always call for provision of additional sensory input. Indeed, decreasing the sensory stimulation that the child is receiving is often the required strategy.

This process of collaboration can be illustrated through our experience with Jessica. Five-month-old Jessica was consistently irritable when her diaper was changed. The reason for this irritability became clear as her mother, Catherine, described the diapering routine. Diapering was usually done on a changing table, filled with a menagerie

> Practitioners should help parents become sensitive observers of their child's sensory strengths and needs.

of stuffed animals that lay under a musical mobile next to a brightly colored mural. Conscientiously attempting to make daily routines occasions for relationship building and brain development, Catherine tried to engage Jessica in active roughhouse play and social games during diapering. However, Jessica was not receptive and fussed. Rather than becoming a fun time of smiles and laughter, diapering had become stressful for both Jessica and Catherine.

After discussing her experience with a developmental specialist during a well child visit, Catherine modified both the physical and social aspects of the diapering routine. She removed the mobile and all but one of the stuffed animals, and she rotated the changing table so that the mural was behind Jessica instead of in her visual range. Catherine also changed her approach to the activity. She valued the social play too much to eliminate it, but she realized that she needed to engage in more gentle play (whispering and subtle smiles instead of loud laughing and sound games). The diapering routine remained "special," but it was much quieter and better suited to Jessica's unique sensory preferences. With some sensitive attention and a bit of guidance from a knowledgeable practitioner, Catherine was able to change her baby's sensory diet and create a better fit between Jessica and her physical and social environments.

Fostering parents' and caregivers' ability to read very young children's behavioral cues, interpret them, and respond contingently is an important part of all infant/family practice. A key concern from the sensory integration perspective is fostering the ability of the parent to read behavioral cues, to interpret them, and to respond contingently to meet the child's sensory needs. Since parent-child relationships are very emotionally laden, the practitioner must demonstrate great care and sensitivity when intervening. Thus practitioners who are concerned with a child's sensory needs can use techniques that are part of the repertoire of many clinicians working with families, including parenting educators, home visitors, early interventionists, and infant-parent psychotherapists. Some suggested strategies are discussed below.

• **"Talking through the baby"** helps parents interpret their child's nonverbal messages. During play or other interactions, the practitioner reflects on what the child may be feeling. "If Johnny could speak, I wonder what he would tell us right now?" "I wonder why he's looking away?" "Do you think Johnny likes it when we pick him up?" "What does that look on his face mean?" "Uh-oh, he didn't seem to like that movement, did he?" These types of questions help the parent to become more empathic with the child— seeing through the child's eyes. The parents become aware of the child's behavioral expressions and their meaning. Talking through the baby affords the practitioner an excellent opportunity to relate the child's sensory experience to behavioral regulation of the "four A's" ("Oh look, don't you think that rocking helped him to wake up and pay attention to you?").

• **Active listening** facilitates insight on the part of the parent as the practitioner repeats or paraphrases what has been said ("So it sounds as if you're feeling that the daycare teacher thinks that Brian is a 'bad kid' because he keeps hitting other children, and that you are a rotten parent.").

• **Direct instruction and modeling** expand the parent's knowledge and skills regarding the child's global development and sensory-based self-regulation. A practitioner may suggest, for example, that there may be reasons why Annie resists sitting in the car seat, beyond the all-too-obvious fact that "she doesn't like it." Annie is very sensory-defensive to movement and touch and finds the car seat very uncomfortable despite the soft lacy pillow that her mother has provided. Once Annie's mother understands the sensory basis for her daughter's resistance, she and the practitioner can discuss how to manage Annie's discomfort by, for example, replacing the pillow with a firm, consistent surface for the seat, changing the technique for putting Annie into the seat, providing a favorite toy for distraction, and removing the lambskin covers on the strapping.

Work with Linda, whose daughter Madeline was described in Chapter 2, illustrates the use of several strategies to promote collaboration.

Linda was aware that she was "not making it" with her baby, and her self-esteem was therefore somewhat fragile. A direct instructional approach could have misfired and increased her feeling of incompetence. The practitioner therefore chose to talk through the baby and engage Linda in general problem solving about sensory-based behaviors. After a period of time, Linda agreed to have a videotape made of one of her play sessions with Madeline. Reviewing the tape was an opportunity for reflective observation and discussion of ways to support Madeline's beginning self-regulatory attempts. In this process, the mother acquired four important insights. First, Madeline was clearly attached to her mother, and they shared an emotionally positive basis for their relationship. Secondly, Madeline's withdrawing behaviors were not rejection, but a reflection of over-stimulation. Third, Linda learned about the very subtle behaviors that Madeline used for self-regulation and communication and how to support them (kneading the blanket, looking away, sucking her tongue). Finally, Linda became better able to grade the sensory input during play and caregiving.

As a result of this intervention, the interactions between Madeline and Linda changed for the better. Madeline was able to engage in play through improved self-regulation of her "four A's," and Linda felt more confident as a parent.

When using this collaborative approach, practitioners should be careful not to overwhelm parents with the jargon of sensory integration. Parents are the experts on their own children. The job of the professional is to provide *additional* information that usefully supplements what parents already know about their babies.

Modifying the environment to grade children's sensory experience

Sensory integrative intervention aims to encourage goodness-of-fit (or just-right challenge) between the child's resources and the sensory-related demands that the physical and social environment place on the child. In order to assess the child's resources, the practitioner needs to consider how the child's sensory diet varies throughout the day, how this variation influences the child's arousal and ability to engage in functional activity, and, eventually, how the diet can be modified to maximize a child's participation in adaptive behavior (Wilbarger & Wilbarger, 1991; Williams & Shellenberger, 1996). After recognizing a child's behavioral pattern and sensory profile, the adult tries to anticipate the child's needs and provides an appropriate sensory diet within a supportive environment.

Reasonably consistent, predictable, and structured daily routines help children self-regulate. Parents and practitioners should anticipate a child's sensory needs. They should not wait until a child is sluggish to introduce an

Proprioception is provided by pushing a baby carriage.

Push-pull activities also provide proioception, but this activity has added tactile input from the sand table.

arousing activity, or wait until a child is overloaded to do something calming. Routines—for example, always telling a child when a transition is going to occur, making sure that storytime always precedes bedtime—can help the child predict what is about to happen and make adjustments for the upcoming sensory changes. Being able to anticipate events enables the child to move from a reactive mode to a purposeful, self-initiated mode of behavior, which, in turn, helps the child cope more successfully with change and sensory perturbations.

When planning a sensory diet, it is important to remember that the effects of sensation on overall organization are variable—no one type of input is *always* calming and organizing or *always* arousing. Table 5.1 lists the visual, auditory, vestibular, tactile, oral-motor, and proprioceptive elements of a sensory diet and their potential effects. When using these types of activities with a child, however, the practitioner should carefully observe for

Table 5.1
Sensory input can be either calming or alerting

Elements	To Calm	To Alert
Visual	Soft or natural colors Muted colors Room dividers, screens Keep visual input steady	Bright lights and colors Move object toward face (looming) Focused lighting on object Move objects at irregular speeds
Sound	Classical music White noises Low-key humming Speak or sing in monotone or slow rhythm	Vary intensity, pitch, or beat Loud music

Vestibular	Rhythmical swinging
	Slow rocking
	Maintaining head or body
	  position
	Sustained movement
		Dysrhythmic or changing speed
		  of movement
		Change position of head
		Rock, jiggle, bounce, or jump
		Upright positioning
		Rotary activities (spinning)

Touch/pressure	Rhythmical patting and
	  stroking (massaging the
	  back)
	Wrap in soft, warm blanket
	Hold firmly for a hug
	Help child stroke plush toy
		Light touch (especially face,
		  palms, and abdomen)
		Gently and quickly rub skin

Oral-motor	Suck on pacifier
	Suck mild flavors
	Induce slow breathing and
	  blowing
	Maintain temperature and
	  texture of food and liquid
		Suck or eat citrus, salty or sour
		  flavors
		Drink cold liquid or frozen pops
		Vary temperature and texture of
		  food
		Chew before or during focused
		  tasks

Proprioception	Resistive activities Rhythmic motor activities	Resistive activities Changeable motor activities

individual responses. These sensory elements influence the child's self-regulation and behavior by modulating the "four A's." For example, tickling, bouncing, and talking animatedly can help a child become more alert. Lowering the lights, slow rhythmic rocking, and whispering may cause the child to calm down and engage in play. One of the central assumptions of sensory integrative theory is that the senses are functionally unified and that input from one modality can modulate or regulate input in another modality (Ayres, 1972; Koomar & Bundy, 1991). Proprioception and pressure touch, in particular, are often used to regulate the more arousing senses such as light touch or vestibular input. For instance, firmly rubbing one's arm after being tickled "erases" the noxious light touch, and engaging in resistive proprioceptive activities (e.g., playing a push-pull game or getting a firm hug) after spinning can help stop dizziness (i.e., disorganization from rotary vestibular input).

One may not see the influence of sensory input immediately because of a possible latency of response and the fact that there is a cumulative effect that builds up over time as discussed in Chapter 1. Since response to sensation builds up over time, a hyperreactive child may be more sensitive to auditory input at the end of a long day than in the morning. In addition, a hyporeactive child may have a latency in responding to sensation that can result in being over-stimulated by a well-meaning adult because of a narrow zone of optimal arousal. Because of this factor, any changes in a child's sensory diet (i.e., the amount or type of sensory input a child is receiving) should be made slowly and conservatively.

Practitioners in the field are continually working with children and families to discover new ways of improving the sensory diet. Patricia Wilbarger, for example, developed a brushing technique to decrease general hypersensitivity or to activate children who are hyporeactive (Wilbarger & Wilbarger, 1991). In this procedure, the adult uses a non-scratchy surgical scrub brush to apply deep pressure, with firm, continuous strokes, to a child's limbs and back. Next, the adult provides joint traction and compression by pulling and pushing the joint surfaces of the child's arms and legs. This tactile and proprioceptive input is quite powerful. Most children enjoy the feeling of being pressure brushed when they are experiencing sensory defensiveness. The procedure, which parents and practitioners can learn under the supervision of a specially trained therapist, takes a few minutes. Pressure brushing is repeated every two hours at first, but the frequency of brushing can be decreased as the child spends longer periods in an organized state. Although numerous practitioners report good results with brushing, the procedure's effectiveness has not been established by clinical research studies.

Like any new therapeutic intervention, the pressure brushing procedure needs to be empirically validated, and

> Any changes in a child's sensory diet should be made slowly and conservatively.

protocols are needed to identify the best candidates for the procedure, optimal frequency and duration of application, specific outcomes to be expected, and longevity of effects. Until research findings are available, experienced practitioners recommend using pressure brushing with caution for children under three, only after other options have been explored. The procedure should not be imposed on a child who finds this sensory input unpleasant and is, of course, not appropriate for children who are medically fragile. Practitioners should also consider the state of the parent-child relationship before offering pressure brushing as an option for parents to implement. The procedure may be experienced as intrusive by a toddler who has begun to demand autonomy or by an insecurely attached child who is in more chronic conflict with the mother; it should not be used when it might place a vulnerable relationship under stress. As always, the practitioner must consider the full range of possible parent-related activities, sensory diet, and environmental adaptation in crafting an intervention approach.

One of the challenges to planning and implementing a sensory diet is to recognize how a child's sensory needs contribute to behavior and other intervention strategies utilized by the treatment team and the family. For example, behavioral techniques are frequently used to manage the behavioral disorganization and stereotypies seen in children with autism spectrum disorders. Behavioral interventions that involve highly adult-directed discrete trials may seem a solution to managing undesired behaviors. However, when a child has major problems in sensory modulation, those techniques that do not consider sensory needs may result in stereotypies that resurface in a different form. Conversely, if an adult responds to inappropriate behavior by providing a positive sensory experience, the behavior will be reinforced instead of extinguished. The key to behavior management in this case is a unified program where the sensory diet activities are presented either on a schedule or before the behavior becomes problematic. If the child engages in an undesired behavior (e.g., biting), the response to that behavior should be based upon learning or behavior theories (Kimball, 1999b).

A sensory diet must fit the child's regulatory needs as they change with different times of the day and in response to different functional contexts. Meals and bedtime are

Crawling through the tunnel provides proprioceptive and vestibular challenges, while shielding the child from the visual stimuli of the large room.

These children are experiencing calming pressure touch while buried in large weighted pillows.

often quite problematic for children with sensory integrative difficulties and require some special planning. Table 5.2 offers suggestions for the care of children who have hypersensitivity or irritability that interferes with their ability to eat a variety of foods or who consistently have difficulty in self-regulation during mealtimes. Table 5.3 offers suggestions for the care of children who have hypersensitivity or irritability that interferes with their ability to go to bed, fall asleep, or self-calm after waking in the night.

A goodness-of-fit can be achieved not only through a graded sensory diet (i.e., influencing the child's senses directly) but also, indirectly, by adapting the physical and social environments (Hanft & Place, 1996; Schaaf & Anzalone, in press). Knowledge of a child's sensory profile helps adults modify the external environment to provide demands that best support interaction and self-regulation. Hyperreactive children need calm settings with minimal distractions and controlled sensory "flow," while hyperoactive children generally do better in a rich sensory environment that provides many opportunities for active sensory-based exploration. Thus the same environment may have quite opposite effects on children with different sensory profiles. An extremely animated teacher or a brightly lit classroom full of mobiles and colorful bulletin boards may easily over-stimulate a child who is hyperreactive, but

Table 5.2
Intervention for Sensory-Related Feeding Disorders

The following suggestions are appropriate for children who have hypersensitivity or irritability that interferes with their ability to eat a variety of foods or who consistently have difficulty in self-regulation during mealtimes:

• Recognize that not all feeding disorders have a sensory basis. Some feeding problems may be due to developmental or medical factors, motor deficits, or emotional disturbances.

• Identify when the sensory-related feeding disorder began. This information can provide insight into the problem. For example, many children have difficulty when changing from pureed to junior foods, whereas others have had longer-standing problems associated with food temperature.

• Consult with the child's health care provider before initiating feeding intervention (e.g., physician, therapist, nutritionist, and/or nurse).

• Consider the complexity of sensory input during feeding. Feeding time should be as distraction-free as possible. Schedule feedings when the adult is relaxed, the child is alert and responsive, and the environment is calm.

• Try to have a predictable routine associated with the beginning and ending of meal times.

• Sensory-related feeding disorders are frequently only one aspect of a more global sensory problem (e.g., hyper- or hyporeactivity). Use calming techniques prior to feeding if the child is over-aroused and hypersensitive. Use alerting techniques if the child is under-aroused and sluggish.

• Introduce changes in food texture slowly. Solids are frequently easier to manage than liquids. They can be thickened with rice, cereal, yogurt, or fruit puree to make them easier to swallow. Variable textures such as junior foods with lumps can be hard to handle due to their inconsistency.

• Children often tolerate more oral stimulation and textures when eating finger foods, as opposed to being fed.

• Avoid foods that have a safety risk, such as nuts, raw carrots, popcorn, and slices of hot dogs. Introduce easily crunchable foods that do not require a lot of chewing, such as Cheerios and cheese curls.

• Use taste and smell to influence reactivity. For example, a toddler who is orally hyposensitive and hypotonic may be effectively aroused when eating a sour pickle.

• Remember that the face is the most sensitive area of the body, so touching in or around the mouth can be very threatening to the child. Minimize nonessential touch.

• Avoid frequent wiping of the mouth during feeding. When you must wipe the face, use a firm pat instead of a light swipe across the mouth, or let the child wipe the face independently.

• Give the child time to close the mouth on the spoon and remove food rather than scraping food off of the upper lip or teeth.

• Position the child in a stable supportive chair during feeding to provide postural stability and to minimize extraneous sensory stimulation (e.g., use a high chair or a chair with an adjustable seat and foot support).

• Recognize that during feeding the rules are different. You may want to work initially on sensory processing problems during nonfeeding times, since nutritional concerns must take precedence during the actual feeding.

• Introduce toothbrushing slowly and playfully. Toothbrushing provides a natural opportunity to work on oral tactile sensitivity. Try Infa-Dent (i.e., a soft finger cot with soft bristles), or a graded sequence of textured, chewable rubber brushes rather than a traditional toothbrush.

• Parents must be centrally involved in all feeding-related interventions. It is best to work within the family's comfort level and style. Make minimal changes in daily routines as you work toward collaboratively agreed-upon goals.

• Respect culturally based feeding practices (e.g., prolonged breast feeding, cradling during feeding).

Table 5.3
Intervention for Sensory-Related Sleeping Problems

The following suggestions are appropriate for children who have hypersensitivity or irritability that interferes with their ability to go to bed, fall asleep, or self-calm after waking in the night.

• Rule out any medical or predominantly psychological reasons for the sleep problem (e.g., reflux, allergies, sleep apnea, teething, parental conflict, extreme dyadic separation issues).

• Gather assessment information, such as the sleep schedule, bedtime and naptime routines, environmental stresses, sleeping arrangements, and the nature of the sleep disturbance.

• Determine how each sensory system supports or interferes with the child's ability to fall asleep and return to sleep after waking. This information helps the parent and practitioner to design interventions that foster self-regulation and modulation of arousal. For example, one infant may require rocking in silence, whereas another infant may benefit from quiet music.

• Increase a regular sleep-wake pattern that promotes nighttime rather than daytime sleep. If the child is taking very long naps, one may gently awaken the child during the day to encourage the need to rest during the night. Be aware of natural biological rhythms in order to know the best times to schedule naps and feedings.

• Recognize that day-night confusion may be a result of a poor fit between the child's self-regulatory capacity and the sensory properties of the day or night environment (e.g., some infants may want to sleep all day and play all night because daytime is too stimulating and they need to "shut down").

• Emphasize calming input in the evening, such as (1) slow linear movement (e.g., forward-back, side-to-side, or vertical head-to-toe rocking and (2) touch pressure (e.g., repetitive firm massage, firm squeezing and releasing of the arms and legs, curling up in a bean bag chair). Do not impose stimulation on a child who finds it aversive, and watch for automatic signs that may indicate sensory overload.

• Put the child into the crib when drowsy but still awake. Thus the child learns to self-soothe to achieve sleep and does not develop the habit of having to fall asleep in the parent's arms.

• Decrease arousing activities before bedtime (e.g., roughhouse). For hypersensitive children, changing the time of bathing or feeding to at least one hour before bedtime can aid in sleep readiness and decrease the tendency toward irritability or spitting up.

• Remember that arousing activity also has social components. Active socialization immediately prior to bedtime can increase separation anxiety and interfere with the child's ability to settle into sleep.

• Support the child's effort at self-calming prior to falling asleep (e.g., provide a pacifier for nonnutritive sucking, build a nest of stuffed animals or pillows to cuddle against, tuck in covers to provide neutral warmth and pressure).

• Assure that the bedding is sensorially compatible with the child (e.g., avoid scratchy or lumpy surfaces). Be sure that the sheets are not cold (e.g., put sheets in dryer, use flannel sheets or sheepskin). Swaddling can also provide natural warmth for relaxation plus the security of a flexed position. The vestibular input from a heated waterbed or inexpensive air mattress may also be beneficial.

• Provide a background of continuous white noise that supports falling and staying asleep (e.g., audiotapes of wind or ocean sounds, humidifier, fan facing away from the child). The continuous sound is better than complete quiet because it masks household sounds and aids the child to fall back asleep after waking in the night. Music boxes that have high frequency sounds are usually contraindicated.

• Attend to the sensory quality of the child's sleep clothing. Some infants may prefer a cotton knit that is tight against the skin and provides touch pressure. Other infants may prefer the opposite—loose-fitting clothes.

• Practice games of separation during the day to help resolve issues related to attachment and autonomy (e.g., peek-a-boo, hide-and-seek). Consider the use of a transitional object during the night as a parental substitute (e.g., teddy bear).

these elements of the social and physical environment may be just what are called for to help the child who is hyporeactive to reach an appropriate threshold.

Parents, caregivers, and practitioners should make themselves more aware of the child's physical environment and its impact on self-regulation and the "four A's." It is important to view the space of the home, childcare setting, or early intervention program from a child's perspective. What would an infant or toddler see and feel in this place? Does the environment support purposeful, self-initiated behavior? Does the environment provide spaces for calming down as well as active exploration? From the adult's perspective, is it an easy and comfortable place to be? Is the environment structured so that adults have time to interact with the child, rather than having to use their time setting up and taking down equipment, or managing the child's behavior? Parents and practitioners need to modify the sensory properties of the child's surroundings so that the physical environment contributes to the child's successful self-regulation, coping, and learning. Table 5.4 provides suggestions for designing the physical environment of the home and group care settings to support behavioral organization in children with different sensory integrative needs.

This activity involves both social and sensory reciprocity as these children try to match their movements to each other.

Table 5.4
Designing the Physical Environment

The following discussion addresses ways to grade the sensory experiences of children in group settings (e.g., child care centers, early intervention programs, community agencies, group home care). Many of the suggestions are also appropriate for adapting the home environment (Merrill, 1990; Zeitlin & Williamson, 1994).

Childproof the environment.

To make the environment physically safe for a child, place gates in front of stairwells, cover electrical outlets, discard broken toys, install window guards, and remove appliances with electric cords that can be pulled off a table. Physical safety is a prerequisite to sensory and motor exploration that supports early motor and cognitive development.

Ensure quality of light.

A mixture of natural light and incandescent lighting is preferred. If fluorescent light is used, the "daylight" or "warm light" fluorescent tubes are recommended for a soft quality of illumination. Fluorescent fixtures should be covered with diffusing screens to prevent glare. Exposed tubes and bare light bulbs should be covered because they cause eyestrain, especially for infants who gaze upward. In general, a diffused light is best so that all areas of the room are equally illuminated. The color of paint also contributes to lighting. Bright white can be too bright while an off-white, yellow, or mauve provides a more calming ambient illumination. Often, classrooms and clinic environments are too bright, resulting in visual fatigue. The degree of illumination can be controlled by a rheostat on the light fixtures and venetian blinds on the windows. The lights can be temporarily dimmed to achieve a calming influence on overly stimulated young children. Direct, glaring sunlight can be avoided by adjusting the blinds to reflect the light off the ceiling.

Ensure quality of heat and ventilation.

Monitor the temperature of rooms, especially at floor level. Be aware of drafts. Recognize that temperature can influence states of arousal and attention. A cold room can increase a child's movement and arousal while limiting attention to learning tasks. An overly warm room can make one sleepy and inattentive.

Monitor degree of environmental stimulation.

Limit clutter, distractions, and extraneous noise. Acoustic tile, drapes, area carpets, and fabric on walls can diminish sound. Close-weave, low-nap carpeting on the floor also helps prevent slipping. Avoid complex wallpaper or long stretches of brightly colored walls; emphasize neutral, soft colors on the walls and ceiling. It is desirable that furniture be child-height and pictures and posters be placed at the general eye level of the children. Decoration should be simple and aesthetically pleasing, with materials readily accessible. It is tempting to display every new project or the artwork of every child, but this practice may be over-stimulating. Areas of the room need to be well defined according to functional use, to enhance a sense of order. For example, specific activities are best allocated to different areas, and particular shelves should be designated to store particular toys. Children then learn where to go to become involved in certain activities and where play materials are located and should be returned after use. A movable screen, or even a small tent, is often helpful to create quiet corners for a particularly distractible or hyperreactive child.

Encourage full use of available space.

There is a tendency for caregivers and young children to crowd together regardless of available space. Adults tend to sit together in group care settings with the infants and toddlers in close proximity. The result is major congestion with inevitable conflicts and clashing of the children. An open-center arrangement is preferred with activity centers, large permanent equipment, and adult furniture distributed around the perimeter of the room. In this way, the children and adults are spread out to allow for one-to-one and small-group interaction (one to three children). Intimate spaces can be created by the arrangement of furniture, shelving units, and low dividers (18" to 40"). This set-up allows children to be in open view of adults but visually separated from other action in the room. This arrangement decreases aimless wandering and over-stimulation. It helps the children organize play and regulate their behavior. Similar structure can be introduced in the home by having a pretend corner, reading corner, and hiding area in a child's bedroom or the family room.

Provide toys and play materials.

Developmentally appropriate toys are an important resource for children. Playthings can range from lavish store-bought toys to the pots, pans, spoons, and discarded boxes and adult clothes that intrigue young children. In addition to these commonly enjoyed playthings, parents and practitioners may select toys and materials that are appropriate to the special needs of a particular infant or toddler. For example, a child with hyperreactivity may respond best to simple basic toys such as hard blocks, whereas a hyporeactive child with poor attending skills may need brightly colored, noise-making toys that provide multisensory experiences. Orange, red, and yellow are particularly stimulating colors, whereas black and yellow offer a sharp visual contrast. A child with hyposensitivity may find lightweight toys difficult to manage; toys of greater weight are easier to handle, such as those made of heavy rubber or wood. For a child with dyspraxia, it is helpful to introduce hammering, playing with squeeze toys, and rolling or pounding Play-Doh. This child can also be provided with the opportunity to play on gross motor equipment, such as rocking boats or horses, large inflatable shapes, slides, and tunnels. Young children enjoy climbing and playground equipment. These activities provide the tactile, proprioceptive and vestibular input that is so critical for sensory modulation and praxis.

About your space . . .

The following questions review some of the environmental factors that can facilitate or inhibit sensory integration and learning.
• Is the child in a stable position that allows his or her hands to be available for manipulative activities?
• Are there auditory distractions that interfere with performance, such as extraneous noise from the street or hallway?
• Are there visual distractions, such as cluttered walls or work surfaces?
• Are the instructional or play materials visually confusing or very complex?
• Is the lighting in the room appropriate to prevent glare?
• Is there available and safe space for active movement and exploration?
• Are there soft as well as hard spaces for children to play in?
• Are there child-accessible places for toys to enable independent clean-up and to minimize distractions?

Direct intervention

Parents and caregivers can do a great deal to provide growth-promoting sensory diets and environments for young children, including those with sensory-based difficulties. To overcome sensory deficits and acquire more adaptive behaviors, some children need the appropriate, graded sensory experiences that are provided only through direct, one-to-one sensory integrative intervention (Ayres, 1972; Koomar & Bundy, 1991; Greenspan, 1992; Parham & Mailloux, 1996). This unique child-directed treatment requires a specialized practitioner such as an occupational therapist. Sensory integrative treatment is best learned in a mentored clinical setting from an experienced practitioner and not through traditional continuing education conferences that rely on lectures.

Individualized direct treatment based on sensory integration theory is often misunderstood (see Table 5.5). Intervention for sensory processing dysfunction involves the provision of enriched sensory experiences, but it is not the same as "sensory stimulation" (Kimball, 1999a; Parham & Mailloux; 1996). Sensory input should be a natural component of activities. All sensory-based activities (especially those that are new to the child) should be active and require an organizing response from the child. Activities are made purposeful when they are linked to the child's affect, intentions, and intrinsic motivation. No matter how rich and stimulating the sensory input, if the activity is not purposeful there is little benefit to the child. This is a clinical challenge when working with very young children who may have less flexibility in their interactions with people and objects in their environment. A similar challenge is seen in children with autism or severe developmental disorders due to limited skills, motivation, or inattention.

> Direct individualized sensory integrative treatment is an art as well as a science.

Direct, individualized sensory integrative treatment is an art as well as a science (Ayres, 1972; Koomar & Bundy, 1991). It is based on the assumption that meaningful sensory experiences can lead to changes in behavior as well as underlying neural processes (Jacobs, Schneider, & Kramer, in press). During assessment of sensory processing, the practitioner hypothesizes about underlying sensory-related reasons for a child's behavioral disorganization, stereotypies, and/or repetitive behaviors. During intervention, the practitioner tests these hypotheses and provides appropriate, graded sensory experiences as a means to help the child acquire more adaptive behavior.

Clinical reasoning is the dynamic process of decision-making that occurs during all intervention. The therapist must synthesize his or her understanding of sensory integrative theory with an evolving understanding of the child's current strengths, needs, and preferences. The goal of the clinical reasoning process, then, is to provide the opportunity for the child to engage in challenging sensory-enriched experiences that are matched to current needs and abilities. Ongoing assessment during intervention is necessary since the child's developmental status, current

Table 5.5
The nature of sensory integrative intervention

Sensory Integrative Intervention is **NOT**	*Sensory Integrative Intervention* **IS**
Sensory stimulation	Sensory enriched
Therapist-directed	Child-directed and relationship-based
Protocol- or curriculum-based	Playful, flexible and dependent upon a specialized environment and a trusting relationship
Passive	Active
Verbally directed	Joint problem solving, experiential and exploratory

level of arousal, and engagement are constantly changing. The practitioner must observe carefully and vigilantly in order to match the therapeutic activity to the child's abilities and needs in the moment and over time.

Since it evolves from the interaction among the practitioner, the child, and the environment, sensory integrative intervention cannot be pre-planned. Instead, the practitioner must choose and grade therapeutic activity by attending continually to four factors: 1) the child's capabilities and motivation; 2) social interactions among the child and adults; 3) sensory input, including modality and properties; and 4) environmental affordances and opportunities (Schaaf & Anzalone, in press). Ideally, when an intervention session is meeting the child's sensory needs through appropriately challenging activities, behavioral disorganization and stereotypies will decrease while organized adaptive behavior increases. Appendix A describes the therapeutic use of play for meaningful engagement of children in sensory-based intervention.

To promote sensory integration, child-directed activities should be emphasized, no matter how simple or unfocused they may initially seem. Imitation of the child's play can provide insight into the sensory properties of the activity and can support social reciprocity. Once the sensory basis of the child's behavior is understood, the practitioner then knows where to begin elaborating on the initial sensory experience and can form ideas about how to introduce alternative activities providing similar sensory input. A common therapeutic error is to make too many changes in activity too quickly. Changes should be small and gradual, and there should be the opportunity for repetition and practice. The child's behavioral response should be monitored to determine if the activity is increasing behavioral complexity and organization or causing the child to withdraw or react in a disorganized manner. One of the most difficult aspects of sensory integrative intervention is allowing the child to direct the activity and to engage in a task long enough for adequate practice and learning to occur. Appendix B provides strategies that the practitioner can use to encourage active involvement and self-initiation by children. These procedures offer alternatives to adult-directed intervention.

Another aspect of child-directed intervention is for the practitioner to determine the communicative intent of the child's behaviors. Children frequently wish to communicate about their sensory needs. Gestures, facial expressions, body postures, signs, or vocalizations suggest how they would like sensory input to be altered—slower, faster, discontinued, more, or less. The child's expression during intervention is often subtle and nonverbal. When these behaviors are responded to contingently, they may become the foundation of social reciprocity—facilitating a social give-and-take between the child and the adult. Engagement in appropriate and organizing sensory-based activities (especially vestibular) can also increase vocalizations (Fisher, Murray, & Bundy, 1991; Frick & Lawton-Shirley, 1994; Ottenbacher, 1982; Ray, King, & Grandin, 1988).

A description of an occupational therapist's work with Luis, a 30-month-old child with hyporeactivity, illustrates the process of clinical reasoning and direct intervention to remediate sensory integrative problems.

When Luis entered the therapy room he was often under-aroused. He did not seem to be aware of changes in the room since his last visit (e.g., the inclined ramp that Elsa, his therapist, had placed right in front of the doorway or a new swing that was hanging in the middle of the room). He merely stood at the door waiting for Elsa or Pilar, his mother, to initiate an activity. At other times (especially when his session followed a medical appointment or other stressful event), he was over-aroused and would aimlessly run around the room squealing.

Any treatment program should be designed to reflect the child's capabilities and needs as understood through standardized and qualitative assessment, but familiarity with the initial evaluation results, alone, is not enough. The clinician must sensitively observe the child as he or she enters *each* session in order to meet the child's immediate self-regulatory needs.

Elsa knew that Luis' underlying problem was hyporeactivity and dyspraxia with resultant limitations in ideation. In order to address these core issues, she first had to help Luis organize his state of arousal and attention. If Luis was under-aroused at the beginning of a session, he would need to participate in some alerting activities (see Table 5.1) such as bouncing on the trampoline or a favorite tickling game. If he was over-aroused and inattentive, proprioceptive activities (such as dragging a large pillow across the room or playing tug-of-war) were a better initial choice.

A therapist must understand the child's individual interests. Luis was difficult to motivate. His ability to explore objects was limited, and he seldom attended to the environment. When intervention began, the only actions that he seemed to like to do were mouthing objects and looking for his mother. These limited interests became the foundation of Luis's treatment. Elsa would give him a toy to mouth briefly, then take the toy away and place it in a succession of different locations around the therapy room. Initially, Elsa chose places that were easy for Luis to reach. As his motor and praxis skills improved, Elsa moved the toys farther away and put them in places that required more complex motor planning to get to. Eventually, Luis was climbing over large pillows or up ramps, through tunnels, or into a wading pool filled with rice or other textured materials to obtain his toys. Elsa knew that he would work hard to reach favorite toys, and she used the toys to motivate sensory-enriched exploration. When Luis was no longer attracted by a particular toy, she would change it or ask his mother to call to him. He never tired of climbing toward his mother for a big hug.

Elsa was using Luis's motivation for a simple activity to progress towards more sophisticated ideation and motor planning. She was also providing the opportunity for vestibular, proprioceptive, and tactile input to improve his sensory modulation and body scheme. Luis had choices, and the activities were child-directed. However, Elsa was guiding his limited choices toward her therapeutic goals. She was modifying the environment to achieve desired outcomes, not directing the activity and telling Luis what to do.

With a child like Luis, motivation is fairly circumscribed. With older children or children with more language or symbolic play, motivation can be more creative. For example, make-believe play around the theme of cooking dinner could be used with one child, whereas another child could "go swimming with the whales" or climb into a pretend tree house. The imagery comes from the children, and the therapeutic guidance comes from the practitioner.

Elsa was also interested in the social interaction that occurred during her sessions. Two aspects of that interaction were particularly important. First, she wanted to make the therapy playful and fun. She wanted Luis to work toward meaningful goals and to repeat the activities over and over again in order to obtain the necessary practice and sensory input. To get that repetition, the activities had to be enjoyable for Luis in an atmosphere of active playful interaction. Secondly, Elsa wanted Luis to trust her. In order to take risks and make developmental changes in the therapeutic situation, children need to be emotionally and physically safe and successful. Emotional safety comes from the interaction between the therapist and child and is based on the practitioner's sensitivity and flexibility.

The practitioner must also form a trusting relationship with the child's parents. The importance of parents to sensory integrative intervention with young children has been discussed throughout this monograph. Even though the target of remediation during direct intervention is the child, it is of primary importance that the therapist collaborate with the parents to discover the child's changing needs and interests. Parents and therapists must engage in ongoing problem-solving about the child's new challenges as he begins to integrate his new abilities into functional contexts beyond the treatment session.

Luis's mother, Pilar, was an integral part of every therapy session. She described the outcome of these sessions as "helping Luis to become a boy." Through the flexible sessions, Pilar began to understand the underlying rationale and goals of the activities and was eventually able to integrate sensory integration into naturally occurring play with Luis and his older brother, as well as help his child care center accommodate to meet his specialized needs.

While treatment was based on Luis's motivation and his relationship with both Elsa and Pilar, the central tool of the intervention was the sensory input provided in the

---

Imagery comes from the children; therapeutic guidance comes from the practitioner.

context of activities. Elsa was always thinking about what types of sensory input Luis was deriving from his activities, how it was influencing his "four A's," and how it could be modified (or sustained) to provide the optimum challenge and sensory input. When thinking about the sensory properties of the activities, Elsa focused on how Luis was reacting to the sensory experience.

As discussed earlier, in Chapter 1, a sensory stimulus may be invariant, but the perception of the stimulus is extremely variable both between individuals and within individuals. That variability is based upon several factors, including what the child has experienced immediately preceding the stimulus, the child's state of arousal, and the child's innate sensory threshold.

For Luis, who had underlying hyporeactivity, spinning—which is a very arousing type of stimulus—might seem like an appropriate choice. However, it was not an option for him. Since Luis had immature postural reactions, he was often frightened by rapid movement that he could not control. At first, Elsa tried some swinging activities with Pilar seated on the swing and holding Luis in her lap. This position gave the boy a secure posture, and Elsa and Pilar initially observed some alerting and a broad smile. As Elsa continued the swinging activity, however, she became concerned when Luis began to flush, yawn, and become sleepy. The swinging was too intense; he was "shutting down." The flushing and sleepiness were signs of autonomic distress and over-stimulation. Elsa discontinued the activity immediately, provided no more vestibular input that day, provided some proprioception through the neck and trunk, and ended the session with some quiet manipulative play. She also asked Pilar to observe Luis closely for the rest of the day. After this experience, Elsa's sessions included less intense vestibular activities that involved more climbing up inclines and climbing in, around, and over obstacles built from sofa pillows and the coffee table. These activities provided both vestibular and proprioceptive sensation and were very organizing for Luis.

Luis's exaggerated response to spinning is not unusual for young children or for children with complex neurological conditions such as cerebral palsy or spina bifida. Practitioners need to be aware of behavioral and autonomic signs of distress that may be associated with over-stimulation; these are listed in Table 5.6. Practitioners who are unfamiliar with autonomic signs of distress, or how to

Table 5.6
Signs of autonomic and behavioral distress in young children

Autonomic	Behavioral
Yawning	Fussing
Sneezing	Crying
Hiccoughing	Grimacing
Sweating	Sighing
Gagging	Startling
Spitting up	Stiffening
Breathing irregularly	Averting gaze
Changing skin color	Pushing away
Abruptly changing state	Arching back
Producing a bowel movement	Staring into space

manage them, should avoid using suspended equipment with very young children or children with documented neurological impairment. Signs of autonomic over-stimulation can often look like sleepiness and thus be mistaken for under-stimulation. When any of the behaviors listed in the table are observed, the practitioner should immediately stop any sensory stimulation and actively engage the child in calming activities. One of the best ways to avoid over-stimulating is to refrain from imposing sensory input on a child. When a child is actively generating vestibular or movement input (e.g., by pumping a swing or climbing up a ramp), the arousing vestibular input is modulated by the calming and organizing proprioception obtained through active resistive movement of the muscles and joints.

Elsa consistently used her knowledge of sensory properties (modalities, intensity, and duration) as she engaged Luis in activities. She knew that he was easily over-stimulated by certain types of input (e.g., high-intensity vestibular stimuli, extreme temperatures, certain smells) but enjoyed others (e.g., light touch, heavy proprioception, gentle bouncing on a trampoline). She also knew that even her knowledge of Luis's individual tolerances and preferences could not always predict his reaction to a given type of input. His response varied according to his current sensory threshold. At the end of a session he was more organized, motivated, and socially available than at the beginning of a session.

The final consideration that Elsa factored into her clin-

The environment for sensory integrative therapy is a specialized place.

ical reasoning was the environment in which she was working. She saw Luis both in his home and in her private office. In her clinic she had much more flexibility to provide graded sensory and motor challenges, since she could readily rearrange the physical space and large equipment (see photograph above). As Luis progressed, Elsa could introduce change—and challenge – into the environment. For example, she created "mountains" and barriers from large, irregularly shaped pillows ("jellos") for Luis to explore as he searched for his favorite toys. As he became more competent, Elsa used more and more of the equipment in the clinic. She even re-introduced certain types of suspended equipment that provided linear (i.e., back and forth) vestibular input without spinning.

By also working with Luis and his family at their home, Elsa could discover how Luis's sensory problems influenced his performance in his natural environment. Pilar worked actively with Elsa to design ways that sensory integrative activities could be incorporated into the boy's play and daily activities. At home, Luis could experience variations of the activities he had learned to enjoy in the clinic. His parents used sofa cushions for the "hide the toy" game and were delighted when Luis began to take pleasure in his backyard swing set.

The therapeutic environment needed for formal sensory integrative intervention is specialized. This setting is required as children get older and can benefit from more flexibility and complexity in treatment (Merrill, 1990). A therapy clinic offers sensory and motor enrichment beyond the capacity of the home setting or a traditional gym or classroom. Of particular importance is the ability to provide vestibular input, which usually necessitates different types of swings and climbing equipment that are suspended from ceiling hooks, and a safe, padded floor surface.[1] The clinician uses climbing equipment, large foam blocks for building, different types of swings, tunnels or barrels, ramps, and scooterboards to introduce new challenges for praxis and sensory-enriched play.

Although it may look to the casual observer like simple, child-directed play, one-on-one intervention with a child with sensory difficulties requires a skilled practitioner and an appropriate therapeutic environment. The practitioner follows the child's lead in terms of specific activities but, at the same time, carefully grades activities with respect to sensory modality, intensity or duration, motor demands, complexity of motor planning, and opportunities for creativity. The practitioner creates a flexible environment and manipulates it to provide a variety of sensory-enriched choices. This process is illustrated in Figure 5.1. Artfully vigilant observation is essential to assure that the child is able to respond adaptively to the sensory input the activities provide. Responses of the child can quickly change from optimally organizing to over-stimulating, and the clinician must anticipate the child's needs and provide calming or organizing activities when necessary. Finally, the therapist must carefully build a trusting yet playful relationship with the child. This relationship is essential to foster the type of risk-taking and sustained activity that is so essential to the process of sensory integrative intervention.

Intervention guidelines

In the following sections we discuss intervention guidelines for children with different sensory modulation profiles and difficulties with praxis. Principles of intervention are presented and illustrated with sample case studies.

---

1. A good source for information regarding the safety of suspension systems is the **Southpaw Ceiling Support Manual** (Southpaw Enterprises, 2000).

Figure 5.1
The clinical reasoning process

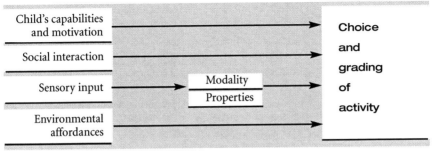

Intervention for children with hyperreactivity

Infants with hyperreactivity have a low sensory threshold, often a narrow band of optimal arousal, and a tendency towards over-activation of the "four A's" (a bias towards a sympathetic autonomic response). Intervention for these children is designed to: 1) decrease or prevent sensory overload and assist modulation of sensory reactivity; 2) achieve an optimal level of arousal and attention; and 3) create a safe and predictable social and physical environment to support more effective engagement.

In order to explore the environment meaningfully, the child with hyperreactivity needs a sense of security and freedom from anxiety. Adults need to be alert for early behavioral and autonomic signs of distress or over-stimulation (see Table 5.6). If the child shows signs of discomfort, the parent or practitioner stops the activity and provides time for recovery. Slowing the pace, rather than stopping the activity, is sufficient for some children who are hypersensitive but not others. Calming techniques can be effective if they are consistent in application. The practitioner needs to stay with one calming activity rather than jumping from one to another. Some examples are downward pressure on the shoulders of the child; bear hugs, with the child facing away from the adult; and engagement in tasks that involve pushing, lifting, and climbing (Grandin, 1992; Zissermann, 1992). Other calming procedures include swaddling (of a very young infant); deep massage; lowering the lights in the room; providing a quiet corner for "cool down"; and listening to tapes of low-frequency white noise, such as sounds of the sea.

The adult must consider the complexity of the sensory input during activities and interactions. Some young children may be able to handle input from only one sensory modality at a time—that is, looking, listening, touching *or* moving, but not two modalities together (Ayres, 1972; Grandin, 1995). Other children may require specific multisensory combinations, such as rocking while being hugged or held. A particularly powerful source of sensory input is eye contact. Therefore, requiring eye contact during an auditory or tactile-based activity may be over-stimulating for some children (e.g., with autism spectrum disorders).

Children with hyperreactivity tend to be irritable. They are hard to be with, and adults need to be aware of their emotional responses to the child's difficult behavior and modulate their own "four A's" in order to avoid over-reacting. The irritability of a child with hyperreactivity may tend to cause the adult to get angry or withdraw. Self-monitoring will help parents and clinicians alike to recognize when they should present appropriate developmental challenges to a child with hyperreactivity, including demands for self-regulation, or more novelty or structure in the environment.

Hypersensitive responses to sensory input are often inconsistent. Because sensory input is cumulative, a child's exaggerated response to a sensory experience may be a result of the whole day's stimulation rather than the challenge just presented. Therefore, the clinician should schedule breaks during the session for recovery and calming, even if the child has not shown intolerance. It is also important to remember that children do not always express hyperreactivity through overt behavior. Some children on sensory overload will shut down and appear inwardly directed, flat, and disconnected.

A description of work with Casey, a child with hyperreactivity, illustrates these concepts and intervention strategies for children with sensory defensiveness.

Ms. Barr and her 16-month-old son, Casey, had recently relocated to a mid-sized city where she had a job opportunity. The mother enrolled her son in an early intervention program at the suggestion of a neighbor, to help her manage his behavioral and developmental problems. She had experienced a succession of pediatricians who attributed Casey's cranky behavior to "chronic colic." Ms. Barr described Casey as "picky and demanding." She said that their relationship was "not easy" and that their recent move only made the situation worse. As a single mother, she felt particularly stressed by Casey's problems with eating, sleeping, and general "willfulness."

Even as a newborn, Casey had been hard to feed, had a poor suck, and gagged frequently. He became a finicky eater who resisted the transition from pureed to junior foods. He now ate a limited selection of finger foods. Casey's sleeping patterns were erratic; he had difficulty staying asleep for any period of time. Casey was highly resistant to strangers and, indeed, was upset whenever anyone except close relatives visited. Consequently, Ms. Barr seldom left her son with a babysitter.

Assessment

During the assessment process, Casey typically demonstrated cautious, inhibited behavior but had episodic periods of fearful crying and tantrums. He seemed to have a very narrow zone of sensory tolerance and poor self-regulation. His irritability and outbursts seemed related to hyperreactivity. From a generally flat, rather disconnected behavioral state, he would go into overload with only a minimal amount of sensory input. Casey seemed as confused by this lack of self-regulation as his mother. To keep the world around him safe and predictable, he acted in a rigid and controlling manner.

At intake, an early childhood special educator was assigned to the family. She functioned in a transdisciplinary manner, supported by the interdisciplinary team of the early intervention program. As part of her assessment, she interviewed Ms. Barr, observed Casey in a variety of contexts, and completed a profile of his sensory diet with his mother. The assessment revealed that Casey could tolerate only limited types of sensory input:

• in the tactile arena, Casey avoided light touch, disliked many textures, and often withdrew from social touch such as a hug;

• visually, he was overly sensitive to bright light and distracted by high-contrast, colorful toys;

• auditorily, he had a startle reaction to high-frequency sounds, was extremely irritable when Ms. Barr vacuumed, and would cover his ears to decrease any loud or sustained sounds; and

• Casey's response to physical movement (i.e., vestibular input) was inconsistent: He craved self-initiated rough-house play yet feared adult-imposed movement.

According to our system of classifying sensory modulation profiles, Casey would be considered hyperreactive. He had a very low and narrow range for modulating his sensory threshold, arousal, and affect. Consequently, he would easily become over-stimulated, get upset, and then have difficulty self-comforting. In the *DC: 0-3* diagnostic system, Casey would be given a primary diagnosis of hypersensitive type regulatory disorder with a fearful and cautious behavioral pattern (Axis I, 401, Type 1).

The developmental assessment revealed relative strengths in Casey's cognitive, expressive, and receptive language skills. He functioned at age expectation for a child of 13-15 months old. Casey was able to communicate through simple words and gestures as long as the tempo of the conversation was unhurried. At these times he could show interest, express his wants, and demonstrate pleasure in interaction. Casey's motor development was typical for a child his age.

Casey's greatest challenge was the influence his sensory modulation problems had on his social-emotional and adaptive development. The mother-child relationship seemed strained due to a poor fit between the partners' temperaments. Ms. Barr was active and intense, while Casey was naturally passive and cautious. Ms. Barr had difficulty reading her son's cues and tended to do too much too fast. His response was to become over-stimulated, cry, and then reject his mother's efforts to console him (which often involved provision of even more sensory input). This pattern often made activities of daily living stressful for all concerned.

Intervention

Intervention with Casey was designed to prevent or decrease sensory overload while simultaneously achieving an optimal degree of arousal and engagement. The special educator focused on enhancing the relationship between Casey and his mother, establishing a sensory diet that promoted self-regulation, and providing therapeutic activities to foster sensory modulation.

Ms. Barr was aware that her relationship with her son was tense. However, she had little awareness of the source of the difficulty. The teacher used three interrelated inter-vention approaches to address the mother-child relation-ship. First, she helped Ms. Barr begin to appreciate Casey's sensory preferences and intolerances through the mecha-nism of designing a sensory diet. By looking systematical-ly at his activities and behavior throughout the day, Ms. Barr started to realize the nature of her son's sensory pro-file and how it related to his problematic behaviors. This discussion led to mutual problem-solving regarding ways to adapt caregiving, daily activities, and play to fit Casey's sensory and behavioral capabilities.

Second, the teacher spent time helping Ms. Barr read and respond appropriately to Casey's cues. Initially, the teacher used the "talk through the baby" technique. She asked open-ended questions about Casey's behavior dur-ing play and social interaction with his mother (e.g., "Does Casey like that?" "What would Casey like to do next?" "What does that expression mean?"). These remarks helped Ms. Barr to slow down her interactions, observe more carefully, and pick up on Casey's moods, gestures, and expressions. In a short period of time, Ms. Barr became quite skillful in relating to and communicating with her son. As her competence developed, she was less prone to over-stimulate Casey, and he was better able to interact warmly with his mother.

The third approach to strengthening the mother-child relationship was honest talk with Ms. Barr about her con-cerns, priorities, and resources. As she developed a trusting relationship with the teacher, Ms. Barr became quite eager to talk about her situation. She was socially isolated, with little support from family or friends. She talked about the following concerns—the lack of a medical diagnosis for Casey, feelings of guilt that Casey's condition was her fault, frustration about his demanding nature, physical exhaus-tion from daily caregiving, and issues related to being a single mother. Information about sensory integration became a part of all these conversations. It was particular-ly helpful to Ms. Barr that Casey's condition stemmed pri-marily from a neurobehavioral rather than a psychological basis. She said, "I thought Casey was this way because I was a bad mother."

Intervention started with Ms. Barr's greatest priorities, which related to Casey's eating, sleeping, and general behavior. The teacher and Ms. Barr planned a number of alterations to Casey's sensory diet that decreased hyperre-

This child is engaged in a high intensity vestibular and proprioceptive activity in the context of a positive social interaction. This might be a good activity to help a hyporeactive child attain threshold.

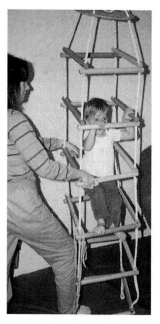

Suspended equipment should be used cautiously with children under three years of

This older child is also engaged in a vestibular and proprioceptive activity in the context of a social interaction. This activity is helpful for a child with poor motor planning or one who is sensory seeking.

activity and enhanced self-regulation, thus making daily routines more pleasant.

• *Feeding:* Ms. Barr used specific calming techniques before mealtimes so that Casey would have a desired arousal level. She developed a clear routine to aid the transition to meals and had Casey carry a weighted stuffed animal to the high chair, thereby providing proprioceptive input. To increase his tolerance of different textures of food, Ms. Barr began by making slight changes in the texture of Casey's favorite foods (e.g., leaving lumps in his mashed potatoes or vegetables). She then gradually introduced new textures and tastes at the same time (e.g., adding small pieces of banana or cooked apple to his cream of wheat). Ms. Barr encouraged Casey to eat chewy finger foods, like bagels. During spoon-feeding, Ms. Barr was careful to give Casey time to close his mouth on the spoon to remove the food rather than scraping food off on his upper lip. She also refrained from wiping Casey's face during meals, since this additional, intense tactile input increased Casey's irritability. Ms. Barr further decreased Casey's oral tactile sensitivity by brushing his teeth with a textured, chewy rubber toothbrush.

• *Sleeping.* Ms. Barr began to use flannel sheets in Casey's crib since they were not scratchy. Casey began to wear tight, cotton-knit pajamas that provided touch pressure against his skin. To calm Casey before bedtime, Ms. Barr would rock him rhythmically and sing quiet lullabies. She would put him in his crib when he was drowsy but still awake, so that he would learn to self-soothe in order to fall asleep. In Casey's bedroom, Ms. Barr played audiotapes of "white" sounds (forest or sea sounds), which helped Casey fall asleep and fall back to sleep after waking.

• *Other routines.* Before intervention began, Casey had been afraid of splashing water and had stiffened his body in resistance to bathing. Now, at bathtime, Ms. Barr started to offer choices, allowing Casey to set the temperature and depth of the water. He also enjoyed the deep-pressure rubbing of the towel when being dried. At other times during the day, Ms. Barr encouraged roughhouse play, rolling, bouncing, hide and seek games, and "horsy"—all gross motor activities that provide proprioception and aid self-regulation and sensory modulation. All of these activities helped Casey to regulate his sensory threshold at an appropriate level and remain in a state of optimal arousal and behavioral organization. They provided somatosensory experiences that inhibited hypersensitivity and discharged physical tension while encouraging Casey to explore his environment actively within the range of his tolerance.

• In addition, Ms. Barr established a predictable, consistent, but flexible daily routine so that Casey would be able to anticipate events and manage transitions. Breaks were scheduled throughout the day to allow Casey to recover from the sensory build-up. Ms. Barr found that Casey could be more successful in social interactions with relatives when she taught them how to slow down questions or invitations to play in order to allow time for Casey to respond.

These intervention strategies and activities had a positive effect on Casey's self-regulation and behavior. As his sensory integration improved, his behavioral rigidity and tendency to overload decreased. And as Ms. Barr implemented Casey's sensory diet, she felt she was getting to know her son better and becoming more comfortable as a parent. This initial period in the early intervention program lasted approximately 6 months. As Casey's self-regulation increased, he made faster and more consistent gains in his developmental skills and became a much happier and independent child.

Intervention for children with hyporeactivity

Infants and young children with hyporeactivity have a high sensory threshold and under-activation of the "four A's" (bias towards a parasympathetic autonomic response). These children may also have a narrow band of optimal arousal since it takes so much sensory input for them to achieve initial threshold. Intervention for these children is designed to: 1) provide sensory experiences that enable the child to achieve and maintain a desired sensory threshold; 2) help the child attain an optimal level of arousal and attention; and 3) support the child's interaction with people and things in the environment.

The child who is hyporeactive needs to be activated in order to engage in more effective exploration, social interaction, or manipulative play. The practitioner may introduce a sensory-enriched environment to provide arousing input to "jump-start" the child. As mentioned earlier, it is essential to make sure that a child *is* indeed hyporeactive before engaging in very arousing activities. If assessment findings are ambiguous, the most effective type of sensory input to begin with is proprioceptive (e.g., bouncing or climbing). The practitioner should provide sensory input in a slow, controlled, systematic manner that brings the child to threshold but not beyond. Too much input can cause the child to become disorganized and even appear hyperreactive. Some sensory input, such as light touch or rapid rotary vestibular stimulation (i.e., spinning), can be very powerful and cause long-lasting and exaggerated responses, including flushing, sweating, sleep disturbances, and appetite changes, hours after the input was provided.

The most organizing and alerting sensory inputs are proprioception and pressure touch, which are low in intensity and have a prolonged influence on the nervous system. These somatosensory inputs can be incorporated into both direct intervention and the activities that make up the child's daily sensory diet. The following arousing activities, which should be directed by the child instead of imposed by the adult, are designed to foster sensorimotor readiness and can be graded based on each child's unique response:

• walking or jumping on a mattress on the floor;

• crawling on and around couch cushions;

• carefully graded swinging or roughhousing;

• climbing on playground equipment; and

• vigorous playful drying after bathtime with a stiff towel.

Some children who have high thresholds may have slow reactions to sensory input. They will react, but gradually. Adults need to provide enough time for the child to plan and initiate a response before they offer additional sensory input. Unfortunately, therapists working with hyporeactive children tend to over-structure sessions, limit time for practice and repetition, introduce too many activities too quickly, and over-direct the child through language. What the child needs, however, is active meaningful engagement rather than passive stimulation. The child's sensory-based needs and motivation must dictate the pacing and activities of sensory-integrative intervention. When motivated, the child is better able to organize, integrate, and use sensory input.

A description of work with Luis, the child with hyperactivity who was described in the section on clinical reasoning, illustrates an integrated intervention program used to address his sensory integrative-related developmental delay and low arousal.

In addition to using one-to-one direct intervention to remediate Luis' underlying sensory modulation problems, the therapist worked with his family to provide an appropriate sensory diet that would assure carryover of therapeutic gains into his daily life. The therapist helped Luis's parents recognize his periods of low arousal and provide experiences that would increase his energy level. The activities recommended for Luis focused on arousing him for engagement while avoiding over-stimulation or disorganization. Luis would become alert after participating in bouncing, roughhouse play, light touch, action songs, and interaction with an animated person. For example, during his bath he could play splashing games, use a loufa sponge, and later dry off with a stiff towel that had not been laundered with fabric softener.

Luis frequently showed a latency in responding to sensation. To avoid over-exciting Luis, adults needed to provide sensory opportunities slowly and carefully. For example, Luis enjoyed bouncing on the trampoline in the morning after his bath. However, too much bouncing caused him to become giggly, silly, and distractible.

Play was a very important focus of intervention with Luis. When children are hyperactive, adults tend to play with them at levels that do not challenge their attentional or cognitive abilities. Luis's parents needed to learn that their son's apparent passivity did not indicate a lack of interest in the world but, rather, an inability to organize action because of poorly regulated arousal and attention. Insight gained through participation in Luis's program was shared with all individuals who were significant in Luis's life (e.g., his older brother, the baby sitter). Special attention was directed to Luis's grandparents, who were very concerned about his lack of motivation.

To help Luis move from simply mouthing objects to more sophisticated play, the therapist first worked with his parents to increase the sensory properties of the toys Luis enjoyed mouthing—for example, adding rough textures, vibration, or a flashing light. Next, the parents learned strategies to facilitate Luis's self-initiation. They learned ways to engage their son and to allow time for him to organize a response. The parents provided cues to start an activity, such as saying, "Ready-set-go," or "What's next?" They also gave him a destination to work toward, by saying, for example, "Put the bear in the box," or "Can I have the bear? He looks like he needs a hug." The parents allowed plenty of time for Luis to act and avoided the tendency to flood him with verbal directions. They became skillful at following his lead in play and imitating his actions before elaborating upon his activity.

Intervention for children with dyspraxia

Intervention for the child with dyspraxia is complex and usually requires a specialized environment and a therapist with advanced training. Readers are encouraged to consult the work of Ayres (1985), Kimball (1999b), Koomar and Bundy (1991), and Parham and Mailloux (1997) for a fuller discussion of intervention for dyspraxia. General principles of intervention to improve the performance of children with dyspraxia relate to which component of praxis is problematic for a child. Intervention may include the following:

• if the child has problems in ideation, the practitioner works to improve sensory modulation and/or the ability to interact flexibly with the environment;

• if the child has problems with motor planning, one works to improve body scheme by increasing tactile and proprioceptive feedback from movement, and to expand the ability to initiate and sequence motor strategies; and

• if the child has problems in executing motor acts, the practitioner integrates practice of motor skills into activities that may also be designed to improve ideation or motor planning.

Therapists work to enhance the child's body awareness and motor control by increasing somatosensory input (i.e., pressure touch, proprioception, and vestibular inputs) through self-selected, resisted, gross motor activities. For example, the child's movements are resisted when he or she is pumping back and forth on a swing or when "helping" to move a heavy beanbag chair. The practitioner joins in child-directed play by imitating the child's activities without asking questions or initiating any demands. The therapist follows the child's lead and allows time for the long latency of response found in some of these children. Rather than suggesting solutions to a novel task during play, the adult provides time for independent problem solving and possibly asks questions about next steps. Gradually the practitioner introduces a change in the environment that requires a modification in the child's play behavior. The child with dyspraxia usually takes longer to learn motor activities than a typically developing child. He or she needs opportunities for repetition and practice, even though, at times, the behavior may appear perseverative.

This child is climbing up a "mountain" that requires motor planning, proprioceptive awareness, and vestibular integration.

The child with dyspraxia needs to be involved in generating goals and planning activities through active engagement in a meaningful, productive activity that emphasizes somatosensory input. The practitioner should avoid too much directiveness, whether verbal or physical. No single activity or group of activities is meaningful, developmentally challenging, or helpful in improving praxis for all children. Praxis is not about the activity or the child in isolation. Instead praxis emerges from the interaction between the child's developmental and sensory integrative capabilities, the child's motivation, and the environmental affordances. For example, searching for a partially hidden object is a praxis-related task for a child with minimal developmental capabilities, problem solving skills, or motivation. The practitioner's task is to create challenges and novelty in the pathway to that object. The adult can hide it under a large pillow, in a container full of balls or rice, or across a room filled with ramps, pillows, and tunnels. For a child who enjoys swinging, the activity that encourages praxis may be getting onto and moving the swing. Still another child may be able to participate in the more complex task of building an obstacle course for exploration. The guiding principle for the practitioner is to modify the environment to provide a motivating, sensory-enriched situation that requires repeated, complex, coordinated action by the child.

This younger child is also using developmentally appropriate motor planning, proprioceptive and vestibular awareness while climbing on an egg crate foam in her own living room.

A description of work with Tanya, a child with dyspraxia, illustrates these concepts and intervention strategies.

At 29 months, Tanya Ellis was an active, curious child. She was initially referred to occupational therapy because of a fine-motor delay. Before her referral to occupational therapy, she was seeing a physical therapist and speech and language pathologist through the early intervention program in her community. Her progress was steady but slower than expected, especially in the gross motor area, where her clumsiness persisted in spite of skilled intervention. Another issue for both the professionals and Mrs. Ellis was the fact that Tanya seldom generalized skills that she had learned to new situations. Mrs. Ellis, in particular, was concerned because Tanya was so inconsistent in what she was able to do. For example, sometimes she was able to play independently with her friends on the climbing structure at her favorite playground. At other times she would watch quietly, unable to keep up with her more vigorous friends. Mrs. Ellis also wondered about the routinized nature of Tanya's play—she tended to do the same things over and over again rather than engage in the more flexible and creative play that is characteristic of children her age.

Tanya was a bit of an enigma to her parents. She had a very strong will. Once she decided she wanted to do something, no person or obstacle could distract her from her goal, and she would accept help from no one. Sometimes, however, she became frustrated easily and promptly called out to her mother for assistance.

Assessment

Tanya's occupational therapy evaluation indicated that she did have a mild fine-motor delay. More importantly, Tanya had dyspraxia, with particular problems in motor planning and body scheme. She was readily able to figure out what she wanted to do—her ideation and motivation were age appropriate—but her motor planning was very poor. Tanya had a poorly developed body scheme. She seemed unaware of where her body was in relation to objects in the environment. For example, she would sit *on* toys instead of next to them and had difficulty positioning her body to sit on a chair. The quality of her gross motor performance (execution) was also poor. She walked with her feet wide apart and her arms overhead in the so-called "high guard" posture. Her torso was stiff, with limited balance reactions. In work with her physical therapist, Tanya was making slow but steady progress in overcoming these problems in execution. The goal of individualized occupational therapy was to work on praxis and fine-motor abilities.

Tanya's occupational therapist, Jed, spent ample time with her parents, helping them to understand how Tanya's dyspraxia contributed to the inconsistency, clumsiness, and frustration that characterized her behavior. Over time, these conversations helped Mr. and Mrs. Ellis to simplify and sequence functional activities to increase Tanya's independence. They also learned ways to encourage generalization of her newly acquired abilities.

Jed felt that Tanya's body scheme should be the primary focus of direct intervention. In order to improve the quality of her motor planning and execution, she needed to have a better idea of the relationship of her body parts to each other and the environment, how it felt to move her body, and how to more effectively sequence movements to achieve a desired outcome. She needed to learn from the sensory feedback involved in repeated movement (i.e., resistive or "heavy work" activities rich in proprioceptive input). Using the clinical reasoning process outlined in Figure 5.1, Jed knew he had to address Tanya's capabilities and motivation, her social relationships, the kind of sensory input that would support change, and the type of environment that could be therapeutically modified.

Intervention

Jed began intervention planning with the environmental opportunities. He chose to provide direct one-to-one therapy in a fully equipped sensory integrative clinic (see p. 93). The space had many hooks in the ceiling from which he could hang various swings, large pillows, ladders, ramps, tunnels, barrels, and tires for exploration. This environment offered creative opportunities to address Tanya's primary sensory integrative problem, her poor body scheme. She needed changing motor activities that generated heavy tactile and proprioceptive input. Through experiencing somatosensory input, she could develop a better body awareness. Jed arranged the environment to offer as much proprioception and change as possible. For example, one week he blocked the entrance to the clinic space with a big pillow that Tanya needed to push or climb over to get into the room. He had the barrel and ramp placed close to a new stretchy fabric swing that was hanging from hooks on the ceiling. This arrangement invited Tanya to crawl, climb, and swing but did not impose activities on her.

Jed's next challenge was to discover ways to enhance Tanya's motivation. He learned, for example, that although she was slow to warm up to the clinic, Tanya enjoyed being a "helper" and pretending to be Super Girl. Jed helped Tanya play out both of these roles through gross motor activities on the equipment. This strategy encouraged both repetition and complexity of activities – for example, Super Girl would fly through the air on the swing as many times as it took to rescue the doggy from the mean witch. Jed was careful to remember that any play ideas had to come from Tanya. She was a curious self-starter who could attend indefinitely to an activity that was her own idea, but she lost interest quickly if an adult tried to impose an activity.

Jed's therapeutic relationship with Tanya developed over time. Tanya needed to trust him, to know that she could have fun with him, and to understand that he liked being with her. Jed needed to be playful, but not childlike, with Tanya. His relationship with Tanya integrated his clinical awareness of Tanya's sensory needs, the environmental challenges, and the play themes important to her. As we have noted, the therapist utilizing sensory integrative theory does not direct or physically manipulate the

> The therapist structures the environment so that the child can make therapeutic choices.

child. Rather, the therapist works indirectly by structuring the environment so that the child can make therapeutic choices. What happens during any given session cannot be clearly anticipated or planned. Although Jed had an idea of what might happen during a session with Tanya, he did not work from an inflexible curriculum.

On one occasion, for example, Jed carefully planned an environmental "invitation" using a large pillow, barrel, ramp, and swing. As it happened, Tanya loved the idea of pushing and pulling the pillow around the room so much that she persisted at this activity for a full 15 minutes. She dragged out more pillows to make a huge "mountain." She then repeatedly climbed up and rolled down her mountain. Although Jed had not anticipated this activity, he encouraged it because it provided both tactile and proprioceptive input, required sequencing and motor planning, and, most importantly, was enjoyable to Tanya. Jed introduced more complexity into the activity by encouraging Tanya to dig some "tunnels" in her mountain and to hunt for buried treasure (dolls and a vibrating ball). Tanya then climbed the mountain as a way of getting into the lycra swing, which had now become a make-believe tree house on top of the mountain. Thus Tanya experienced rich somatosensory input and complex motor planning within a spontaneous, self-motivated activity sequence. Jed's challenge was to keep these underlying intervention goals in mind while refraining from imposing his structure on the sessions.

Summary

This chapter on intervention emphasizes the importance of collaborative work with parents and modification of the environment to grade children's sensory experiences. A goal is to attain a goodness-of-fit between the sensory-related demands of the physical and social environments and the child's resources. A well-balanced sensory diet can facilitate the achievement of a good fit. Direct one-to-one intervention can also be provided based on principles of sensory integrative theory and clinical reasoning. Lastly, case studies illustrate intervention activities for children with different sensory modulation profiles and difficulties with praxis.

Play in the Context of Sensory-Based Intervention

Play is a critical activity for self-regulation and self-expression. It provides an opportunity for the child to organize thoughts, feelings, and skills within the context of discovering the new and making sense of the familiar. Play integrates the child's internal and external worlds. It is a spontaneous, voluntary involvement that is initiated and regulated by the child. The acts of play are performed for their own intrinsic reward. Because the child is in command, the constraints of reality can be ignored for free expression of emotions, fantasy, and imagination. However, sensory problems may interfere with the development and expression of various types of play behaviors in the young child.

Within professional practice, play can serve as a medium for remediation of specific sensory-processing deficits. The practitioner can create a play milieu that encourages sensory integration and the acquisition of developmentally appropriate skills in an emotionally rich environment. Therapeutic and educational intervention that fails to appreciate this natural drive to play can result in distress, resistance, or boredom by the child. Play also provides the motivation and drive that often enables children to tolerate increasing amounts of sensory input. For example, the child with tactile defensiveness may be intolerant of touch while getting dressed but may readily tolerate the same tactile stimulus when engaged in a pretend play situation with his or her best friend. The following discussion highlights issues that are related to body-oriented play, manual or manipulative play, symbolic or dramatic play, and social play with peers (Lindner, 1993; Parham & Fazio,

1997; Schaefer, Gitlin-Weiner, & Sandgrund, 2000; Schaaf, Merrill, & Kinsella, 1987; Zeitlin & Williamson, 1994).

Body-oriented play

Early play behavior tends to focus on the body. The infant enjoys patting, scratching, and looking at body parts; plucking clothes; kicking the legs and rubbing them together; and eventually sucking on the toes and rocking in various positions. Often, children with sensory integrative deficits do not experience or enjoy this exploration. They may have poor muscle tone, sensory discomfort, poverty of movement, and disorganization associated with problems in sensory processing. Body-based play is particularly important for older children with motor planning problems who have a faulty body schema. Likewise, somatosensory exploration is essential for children with a disorder in sensory modulation. They need pushing, pulling, lifting, climbing, and carrying activities that offer resistive movement.

The following sample activities promote self-awareness and body-oriented play in the young child:

• Rub the child's body with lotion, powder, or materials of different textures (e.g., sponge, towel). This activity can be incorporated quite naturally in the home during bathing and diapering. Be careful not to impose this type of stimulation on the child but, rather, integrate it into naturally occurring social play.

• Encourage the infant to play with his or her legs in hand-to-knee, hand-to-foot, foot-to-mouth, and foot-to-foot patterns. Simple action songs with the feet can be introduced, such as "This Little Piggy Went to Market." Other songs that usually involve the arms can also be played with the legs. (e.g., "Pat-a-Cake," "So Big," "The Itsy, Bitsy Spider"). Recognize that a child with hyperreactivity may be better able to tolerate self-touch than being touched by others. These games can provide a powerful way to introduce emotionally safe touch.

• For a young child with hyporeactivity, tie a ribbon and bell around the child's wrist or ankles so that movement of the limbs creates auditory and visual feedback.

• Emphasize gross motor experiences, such as rolling, bouncing, and "rough-housing" within the range of the child's tolerance. Be careful to avoid disorganized responses or abnormal postures. For example, if the child is bounced while straddling the adult's lap or leg (playing "horsy"), the head and trunk should be in erect alignment with the hips flexed so that the child experiences normal extension patterns against gravity during the bouncing movement. In contrast, bouncing a child who has cerebral palsy and spasticity on his feet can contribute to abnormal postures, even though it may provide organizing sensory input.

Manual play

Playing noisily with objects is common among young children, particularly after 4-5 months of age (Belsky & Most, 1981). A sensory deficit may limit the coordinated use of the arms necessary to acquire a wide repertoire of play schemes. Therefore, intervention must facilitate not only fine motor skills but the sensorimotor body schema that supports manual play. Initially, spoons and plastic keys encourage banging, hitting, and shaking. Enjoyable activities that foster more sophisticated motor actions include crumbling and tearing paper, playing with a busy box, pulling tissues from a box, and pushing toy cars. The ability to combine objects in play is promoted through putting objects into containers and emptying them out, pulling apart or putting together pop beads, stacking blocks, and stringing beads to wear as a necklace.

From an early age, the child with poor sensory processing needs experiences that involve the integration of the two sides of the body. One aspect of this bilateral integration is the simultaneous use of both hands. Bilateral reach and grasp are provided by large toys, such as balls and cuddly animals, as well as "hold-on" toys, such as rocking horses, riding cars with steering wheels, and push toys (e.g., doll carriage, toy lawnmower). These activities are rich in the somatosensory input necessary for developing praxis. Likewise, many musical toys involve two hands, such as cymbals, drums, and triangles.

Symbolic play

The development of symbolic or dramatic play is particularly crucial for children with limited processing abilities. It provides an opportunity to manifest thoughts and emotions through activities. Symbolic play provides a natural outlet for the expression of themes related to control, fear, anxiety, dependency, aggression, and loss. When sensory integrative goals are integrated into pretend play during intervention, the child is motivated and engaged. The focus for the child is the personally meaningful expression of affect. The management of increased sensory and praxis demands is an underlying corollary to play. Of course, children with sensory integrative problems have a great need for activities that provide both an emotional release and an opportunity for the positive building of self-esteem.

Some children tend to stay at a rather concrete level of play, such as combining common objects together (e.g., using a brush to comb the hair). Through modeling and elaboration, the practitioner or parent can extend the play content to a more representational and dramatic level. Intervention should initially emphasize helping the child pretend actions that involve the self and later pretending with a doll or the adult. With time, the child is assisted to use one object to represent another. Early symbolic play can be encouraged by playing with spoons, cups, and plates to model stirring, dishing out food, drinking, eating, or blowing on hot food. Washing and drying the dishes can also be a part of the play sequence. Imaginative play situations may incorporate the use of stuffed animals, puppets, and miniature people with accompanying environments that represent the home, gas station, or school. Likewise, pretend play episodes may entail dressing up, going to the moon, having a tea party, and playing house.

Social play with peers

In typical development of social interaction with peers, the very young child initially observes the play of others or plays in parallel fashion beside other children. During the toddler period there is a lot of imitation of the movements and positions of other children (e.g., one child squats, runs, or climbs, and the other children follow).

Over time, the child engages in associative play in which there is talking and toy sharing, but the children have separate play agendas (e.g., they are involved in different activities in the play house). Gradually, more cooperative play emerges with the children's playing together in a goal-oriented manner with a common end. This more advanced level of play evolves into the ability to participate in games with pre-established rules.

For some children, it is a challenge to progress through these various developmental stages. Problems in sensory integration, communication, or coordination make it difficult to keep up with the social exchange and shifting pace that should occur naturally during play sequences with peers. As a result, there is a tendency for some of these children to prefer solitary play, to assume a passive role of watching others, or to prefer playing with adults or significantly younger children.

A goal of intervention, therefore, is to assist children with special needs to acquire more sophisticated skills in social interaction with peers. Typically, such experiences are provided through circle time and other group activities. It is also beneficial to cluster children together in pairs or small groups during occupational, physical, and speech-language therapy sessions. Many children become more expressive and actively involved in these situations than in adult-child individual therapy. Interacting with other children is highly motivating and may provide valuable modeling during difficult activities.

In pairs or small groups, children begin to develop an awareness of the feelings of others; they learn how to be a friend, and they learn to help each other. The adult can foster this development by labeling moods and reactions of the children and encouraging them to assist one another in completing activities. For instance, the child with dyspraxia can learn to ask a friend to retrieve a toy that has fallen from reach instead of always relying on adult assistance. Thus, the child acquires the self-initiated coping ability to balance independence with necessary dependence on others.

It is also important, however, to encourage social engagement with peers during movement-oriented activities. Movement experiences can be selected in accordance with the child's ability and modified according to the disability. Obstacle courses can be created with the children in which they maneuver under, over, up, and through objects in the environment by rolling or crawling in the all-fours position. Circle games may include "Simon Says," which uses the limbs to imitate different movement patterns; action songs such as "Wheels on the Bus"; and bouncing balloons or foam balls on a large sheet shaken by the children to make "popcorn."

Strategies To Enhance Self-Initiation and Adaptive Behavior

This monograph emphasizes the importance of a child's being self-directed in order to enhance sensory integration and self-regulation. It is often difficult, however, for the adult to avoid a directive instructional style that places the child in a reactive role. The adult gives directions and models the task, the child responds, and the adult then reinforces the behavior. There is little opportunity for the child to be self-initiating, to modulate the sensory systems, or to motor plan. The strategies described below promote more reciprocity in the relationship and autonomous action on the part of the young child. These strategies create an environment that challenges the child, makes demands in an indirect way, and encourages problem solving (Bricker & Cripe, 1992; Greenspan & Wieder, 1999; Zeitlin & Williamson, 1994).

Indirect intervention strategies

Indirect intervention strategies influence the child's behavior through management of space, materials, equipment, and individuals in the surroundings. Direct intervention strategies influence the child's behavior through specific interaction with the adult (e.g., modeling, verbal guidance, physical prompting). In most cases, some combination of direct and indirect strategies is indicated for a child. Care needs to be taken, however, to avoid over-reliance on direct intervention strategies since they may reinforce a passive, dependent coping style. Direct strategies may predominate at the beginning of an intervention program with a gradual shifting to more indirect strategies as the child progresses and approaches discharge from services.

Preview and review

Many children with sensory integrative deficits are highly reactive to the world around them—fearing change, disorganized during transitions, and experiencing sensory overload. They have limited self-initiation. These children can learn to anticipate events and to try new behaviors on their own when there is a brief preview of the steps of the task before beginning the activity. A similar review is performed on completion of the activity. This intervention strategy not only encourages greater understanding and participation, but it also helps the child internalize a structure for addressing other similar tasks. Previewing the schedule of the day helps children establish a routine and prepare for next steps. Reviewing the schedule assists them to make sense and order out of what has happened.

Set-up and clean-up

Children learn how to participate actively in a situation when they have some part in preparing for an activity and helping to clean up afterward. By having a role in an activity, children take responsibility and are not merely passive recipients. For example, a child may be asked to bring certain materials to the activity area and to return them when finished. The sensory demands of set-up and clean-up are highly variable, depending on how the practitioner structures the task. Involving children in set-up and clean-up has the additional advantage of providing organizing proprioceptive input at transitions, which are often times of potential disorganization. The proprioception provides a calming sensory input, at the same time as providing cognitive and emotional support for transitioning.

Novelty and familiarity

Introduction of a new toy or activity may stimulate some children to try new behaviors. Skillful grading of novelty is particularly important for adapting the sensory threshold of children who are impulsive, hyperactive, or withdrawn. For other children, the use of a familiar toy or activity may provide the necessary security and sensory sameness to foster participation. Practitioners and parents need to moderate the degree of novelty and familiarity based on the sensory status and coping style of the child. For instance, an accessible bookcase could have shelves for familiar and novel toys. The novel toys are rotated on a regular basis. Depending on interest or need for self-regulation, the child can choose a comforting familiar toy or a new stimulating one. Novelty is an important factor that should be used when working with children with sensory modulation issues. For example, introduction of novelty can be a powerful alerting force in the hyporeactive child. One can introduce moderate novelty into his or her environment to encourage orientation and attention.

Planned forgetting

The adult encourages the child to seek the missing element by omitting an important action or material in a familiar activity. For example, the adult may not set out the juice at snack time or may present the child with only one glove of a pair. The child is encouraged to ask questions or seek some appropriate solution.

Omitting or changing a familiar step

When an adult does not do what is expected, children are stimulated to recognize the unusual or omitted action, ask the adult about it, or find some innovative solution. When using this intervention strategy with a young child, the chosen behavior may border on the absurd (e.g., putting a diaper on the foot or combing the hair with sunglasses).

Piece by piece

The piece-by-piece strategy can be used when an activity has material that includes many pieces (e.g., a puzzle, food, blocks). The child is encouraged to ask for each piece as needed, thereby setting his or her own pace and taking responsibility for completing the task. This strategy is particularly helpful to promote social interaction.

Visible but unreachable

The placement of a desired object out of reach but within sight encourages problem solving. The child may have to retrieve it independently or learn to ask for assistance. This strategy is particularly useful for the child with motor planning difficulties.

Adult assistance

With the use of materials or activities that require adult assistance, the child learns to ask for help when needed—

for example, giving the child a toy that has a lid that is too complex to open independently. Assistance needs to be carefully graded to promote self-regulation and self-reliance.

Watch, wait, and wonder

This phrase is commonly used to remind parents and practitioners to observe the child closely before acting. Instead of taking sufficient time to watch a child in the context of the environment to judge what is happening, adults are prone to jump in and take over. As a result, the child is not given adequate time to interact in a self-directed, generative way. This is especially true for children who have trouble modulating their sensory threshold or who have dyspraxia. The child with hyporeactivity requires more time to notice the problem, while the child with hyperreactivity may need time to approach a novel situation. The child with dyspraxia may require more time to plan a strategy for action. Interaction on "adult time" may be too fast-paced for many children who are functioning on the slower tempo of "child time."

Cues to start

Some children have difficulty initiating or continuing an action due to passivity or problems in praxis—especially planning and sequencing steps. They may need a cue to start an activity and one to help them know what to do next. Such alerting cues can be provided in numerous ways: (1) saying "Ready, set, go!"; (2) asking "What's next?"; (3) tapping the child's arm as a physical prompt; (4) saying "Uh-oh," which cautions the child that there is "trouble"; and (5) putting objects in the child's hand, indicating that it is his or her turn.

Promote undoing

Some children with sensory deficits insist on rigid routines and are difficult to engage. If the practitioner changes something in their play, they will undo what was done and put it back as before. For example, moving a block out of line will cause the child to "correct it" by putting it back in position. If the adult makes a "mistake" by parking the toy truck outside the garage, the child will undo the error by placing it in the garage. The act of undoing is developmentally easier for the child than generating a new, purposeful act. One should build this technique on something the child is spontaneously doing and implement it in a positive, nonconfrontational manner.

Stages of learning

The first stages of learning are acquisition of a skill and the ability to maintain the new learning. The next stages are achieving mastery and generalization (i.e., becoming proficient in the skill across a variety of situations). Children acquire new skills, become fluent in performing skills, and learn to generalize skills through repetitive practice during play. There is a tendency, however, to focus on the acquisition of a new skill and to allow inadequate opportunity to practice the skill until it becomes truly integrated. Sensory integrative intervention emphasizes practice and repetition through its focus on child-directed engagement in meaningful activity and play.

Target for movement

Motor planning is easiest when the child has an end point for the action. All of these actions have a destination that organizes the movement—putting a piece in a puzzle, dumping objects into a container, or throwing bean bags at a target. Providing a destination for the action helps the child to plan, initiate and sequence the movement patterns.

References

Als, H. (1986). A synactive model of neonatal behavioral organization: Framework for the assessment of neurobehavioral development in the premature infant and for support of infants and parents in the neonatal intensive care environment. *Physical & Occupational Therapy in Pediatrics, 6,* 3-53.

Als, H. (1982). Toward a synactive theory of development: Promise for the assessment and support of infant individuality. *Infant Mental Health Journal, 3,* 229-243.

Als, H. (1989). Self-regulation and motor development in preterm infants. In J. Lockman, & N. Hazen (Eds.). *Action in social context: Perspectives on early development* (pp. 65-97). New York: Plenum Press.

Anzalone, M.E. (1993). Sensory contributions to action: A sensory integrative approach. *Zero to Three, 14*(2), 17-20.

Anzalone, M.E., & Williamson, G.G. (2000). Sensory processing and motor performance in autistic spectrum disorders. In A. Wetherby & B. Prizant (Eds.) *Communication and language issues in autism and pervasive developmental disabilities: A transactional developmental perspective.* Baltimore: Brookes.

Ayres, A.J. (1972). *Sensory integration and learning disabilities.* Los Angeles: Western Psychological Services.

Ayres, A.J. (1979). *Sensory integration and the child.* Los Angeles: Western Psychological Services.

Ayres, A.J., (1985). *Developmental dyspraxia and adult onset apraxia.* Torrance, CA: Sensory Integration International.

Ayres, A.J., 1989. *Sensory integration and praxis tests.* Los Angeles: Western Psychological Corporation.

Baranek, G.T. (1999). Autism during infancy: A retrospective video analysis of sensory-motor and social behaviors at 9-12 months of age. *Journal of Autism and Developmental Disorders, 29,* 213-224.

Baranek, G.T., Foster, L.G., & Berkson, G. (1997a). Sensory defensiveness in persons with developmental disabilities. *Occupational Therapy Journal of Research, 17,* 173-185.

Baranek, G.T., Foster, L.G., & Berkson, G. (1997b). Tactile defensiveness and stereotyped behaviors. *American Journal of Occupational Therapy, 51,* 91-95.

Belsky, J., & Most, R.K. (1981). From exploration to play: A crosssectional study of infant free play behavior. *Developmental Psychology, 17,* 630-639.

Berg, W.K., & Berg, K.M. (1979). Psychophysiological development in infancy: State, sensory function, and attention. In J. Osofsky (Ed.), *Handbook of Infant Development* (pp. 238-317). New York: J. Wiley and Sons.

Brazelton, T. B. (1990). Saving the bathwater. *Child Development, 61,* 1661-1671.

Brazelton, T. B. (1992). *Touchpoints: Your child's emotional and behavioral development.* Reading, MA: Addison-Wesley Publishing Company.

Brazelton, T.B. (1984). *Neonatal Behavioral Assessment Scale, 2nd Edition, Clinics in Developmental Medicine, No. 88.* Philadelphia: J.B. Lippincott.

Bricker, D., & Cripe, J.J.W. (1992). *An activity-based approach to early intervention.* Baltimore: Brookes.

Bundy, A. C. (1991). Play theory and sensory integration. . In A.G. Fisher, E.A. Murray & A.C. Bundy (Eds.), *Sensory integration: Theory and practice* (pp. 46-68). Philadelphia: F.A. Davis.

Burke, J.P. (1998). Play: The life role of the infant and young child. In J. Case-Smith (Ed.), *Pediatric occupational therapy and early intervention* (2nd ed.) (pp. 189-206). Boston: Butterworth-Heinemann.

Cermak, S.A. (1988). The relationship between attention deficit and sensory integration disorders (Part 1). *American Occupational Therapy Association Sensory Integration Special Interest Section Newsletter, 11*(9), 1-4.

Cermak, S.A. (1991). Somatodyspraxia. In A.G. Fisher, E.A. Murray & A.C. Bundy (Eds.), *Sensory integration: Theory and practice* (pp. 137-171). Philadelphia: F.A. Davis.

Chess, S., & Thomas, A. (1986). *Temperament in clinical practice.* New York: Guilford Press.

Cook, D.G. (1991). The assessment process. In W. Dunn (Ed.). *Pediatric occupational therapy: Facilitating effective service provision* (pp. 35-73). Thorofare, NJ: Slack.

Coster, W. (1998). Occupation-centered assessment of children. *American Journal of Occupational Therapy, 52,* 337-344.

Cynkin, S., & Robinson, A.M. (1990). *Occupational therapy and activities health: Toward health through activities.* Boston: Little, Brown.

DeGangi, G.A., Wietlisbach, S., Goodin, M., & Scheiner, N. (1993). A comparison of structured sensorimotor therapy and child-centered activity in the treatment of preschool children with sensorimotor problems. *American Journal of Occupational Therapy, 47,* 777-786.

DeGangi, G.A., & Balzer-Martin, L.A. (1999). The sensorimotor history questionnaire for preschoolers. *Journal of Developmental and Learning Disorders, 3*(1), 59-83.

DeGangi, G.A., & Greenspan, S. (1989). *Test of Sensory Functions in Infants.* Los Angeles: Western Psychological Services.

DeGangi, G.A., & Poisson, S. (1995). *Infant and Toddler Symptom Checklist.* San Antonio, TX: Therapy Skill Builders.

Dunn, W. & Westman, K. (1997). The sensory profile: The performance of a national sample of children without disabilities. *American Journal of Occupational Therapy, 51,* 25-34.

Dunn, W. (1997). The impact of sensory processing abilities on the daily lives of young children and their families: A conceptual model. *Infants and Young Children, 9,* 23-35.

Dunn, W. (1999). *Sensory Profile.* San Antonio, TX: Psychological Corporation.

Dunn, W., & Brown, C. (1997). Factor analysis on a sensory profile from a national sample of children without disabilities. *American Journal of Occupational Therapy, 51,* 490-499.

Dunn, W., Brown, C., & McGuigan, A. (1994). The ecology of human performance: A framework for considering the effect of context. *American Journal of Occupational Therapy, 48,* 595-607.

Fisher, A.G., Murray, E.A., & Bundy, A.C. (Eds.) (1991). *Sensory integration: Theory and practice.* Philadelphia: F.A. Davis Co.

Frick, S.M., & Lawton-Shirley, N. (1994). Auditory integrative training from a sensory integrative perspective. *American Occupational Therapy Association Sensory Integration Special Interest Section Newsletter, 17,* 1-3.

Gibson, E.J. (1988). Exploratory behavior in the development of perceiving, acting, and the acquiring of knowledge. *Annual Review of Psychology, 39,* 141.

Grandin, T. (1995). *Thinking in pictures.* New York: Doubleday.

Grandin, T. (1992). Calming effects of deep touch pressure in patients with autistic disorder, college students, and animals. *Journal of Child and Adolescent Psychopharmacology, 2,* 63-72.

Greenspan, S. (1992). *Infancy and early childhood: The practice of clinical assessment and intervention with emotional and developmental challenges.* Madison, CT: International Universities Press.

Greenspan, S.I. & Wieder, S. (1999). *The child with special needs: Emotional and intellectual.* Reading, MA: Addison-Wesley.

Greenspan, S.I., & Meisels, S.J. (1996). Toward a new vision for the developmental assessment of infants and young children. In S.J. Meisels & E. Fenichel (Eds.), *New visions for the developmental assessment of infants and young children* (pp. 11-26). Washington, D.C.: ZERO TO THREE

Hanft, B.E., & Place, P.A. (1996). *The consulting therapist: A guide for OTs and PTs in schools.* San Antonio: Therapy Skill Builders.

Holloway, E. (1998). Early emotional development and sensory processing. In J. Case-Smith (Ed.), *Pediatric occupational therapy and early intervention* (2nd ed.) (pp. 167-187). Boston: Butterworth-Heinemann.

Jacobs, S.E., Schneider, M.L., & Kraemer, G.W. (in press). Environment, neuroplasticity and attachment: Implications for sensory integration. In E. Blanche, R. C. Schaaf, & S.S. Roley (Eds.). *Sensory integration and developmental disabilities.* San Antonio, TX: Therapy Skill Builders.

Kagan, J. (1997). Temperament. In S. Greenspan, S. Wieder, & J. Osofsky (Eds.), *Handbook of child and adolescent Psychiatry: Infants and Preschoolers: Development and syndromes, Volume 1* (pp. 268-275). New York: John Wiley.

Kandel, E.R., Schwartz, J.H., & Jessell, T.M. (2000). *Principles of Neural Science* (4th ed.). New York: McGraw-Hill.

Kientz, M.A., & Dunn, W. (1997). A comparison of the performance of children with and without autism on the sensory profile. *American Journal of Occupational Therapy, 51,* 530-537.

Kimball, J.G. (1999a). Sensory integration frame of reference: Theoretical base, function/dysfunction continua, and guide to evaluation. In P. Kramer & J. Hinojosa (Eds.), *Frames of reference for pediatric occupational therapy* (2nd ed.) (pp. 119-168). Philadelphia: Lippincott, Williams, & Wilkins.

Kimball, J.G. (1999b). Sensory integration frame of reference: Postulates regarding change and application to practice. In P. Kramer & J. Hinojosa (Eds.), *Frames of reference for pediatric occupational therapy* (2nd ed.) (pp. 169-204). Philadelphia: Lippincott, Williams, & Wilkins.

Knickerbocker, B.M. (1980). *A holistic approach to the treatment of learning disorders.* Thorofare, NJ: Slack, Inc.

Koomar, J.A. (1996). *Vestibular dysfunction is associated with anxiety rather than behavioral inhibition or shyness.* Unpublished doctoral dissertation. Boston University. Boston, MA.

Koomar, J.A., & Bundy, A.C. (1991). The art and science of creating direct intervention from theory. In A.G. Fisher, E.A. Murray, & A.C. Bundy (Eds.), *Sensory integration theory and practice* (pp. 251-314). Philadelphia: F.A. Davis Company.

Kopp, Claire B. (1982). Antecedents of self-regulation: A developmental perspective. *Developmental Psychology,18,* 199-214.

Lester, B.M., Freier, K., & LaGasse, L. (1995). Prenatal cocaine exposure and child outcome: What do we really know. In M. Lewis & M. Bendersky (Eds.), *Mothers, babies, and cocaine: The role of toxins in development* (pp. 19-40). Hillsdale, NJ: Erlbaum.

Lewkowicz, D.J., & Lickliter, R. (1994). *The development of intersensory perception: Comparative perspectives.* Hillsdale, NJ: Erlbaum.

Lezak, M.D. (1995). *Neuropsychological assessment* (3rd ed.). New York: Oxford University Press.

Lieberman, A., Wieder, S., & Fenichel, E. (Eds.) (1997). *The DC: 0-3 Casebook.* Washington, D.C.: ZERO TO THREE.

Lindner, T.W. (1993). *Transdisciplinary play-based intervention: Guidelines for developing a meaningful curriculum for young children.* Baltimore: Brookes.

McIntosh, D.M., Miller, L.J., Shyu, V., & Hagerman, R.J. (1999). Sensory-modulation disruption, electrodermal responses, and functional behaviors. *Developmental Medicine and Child Neurology, 31,* 608-615.

McIntosh, D.N., Miller, L.J., & Shyu, V. & Dunn (1999). Overview of the Short Sensory Profile. In W. Dunn, *The Sensory Profile: User's manual.* San Antonio, TX: Psychological Corporation.

Merrill, S.C. (Ed.) (1990). *Environment: Implications for occupational therapy practice in sensory integration.* Rockville, MD: American Occupational Therapy Association.

Miller, L.J. (1988). *Miller Assessment of Preschoolers.* San Antonio, TX: Psychological Corporation.

Ottenbacher, K. (1982). Sensory integration therapy: Affect or Effect. *American Journal of Occupational Therapy, 36,* 571-578.

Parham, L.D., & Fazio, L.S. (1997). *Play in occupational therapy for children.* St. Louis, MO: Mosby.

Parham, L.D., & Mailloux, Z. (1996). Sensory integration. In J. Case-Smith, A.S. Allen, & P.N. Pratt (Eds.), *Occupational therapy for children* (3rd ed.) (pp. 307-356). St. Louis: Mosby.

Ray, T., King, L.J., & Grandin, T. (1988). The effectiveness of self-initiated vestibular stimulation in producing speech sounds in an autistic child. *Occupational Therapy Journal of Research, 8,* 186-190.

Rothbart, M.K., & Derryberry, D. (1981). Development of individual differences in temperament. In M.E. Lamb & A.L. Brown (Eds.), *Advances in developmental psychology* (pp. 383400). New York: Medical and Scientific Books.

Royeen, C.B., & Lane, S.J. (1991). Tactile processing and sensory defensiveness. In A.G. Fisher, E.A. Murray, & A.C. Bundy, (Eds.), *Sensory integration: Theory and practice* (pp. 108-131). Philadelphia: F.A. Davis Co.

Schaaf, R.C., & Anzalone, M.E. (in press). Sensory integration with high-risk infants and young children. In E. Blanche, R. C. Schaaf, & S.S. Roley (Eds.). *Sensory integration and developmental disabilities.* San Antonio, TX: Therapy Skill Builders.

Schaaf, R.C., Merrill, S.C., & Kinsella, N. (1987). Sensory integration and play behavior: A case study of the effectiveness of occupational therapy using sensory integrative techniques. *Occupational Therapy in Health Care, 4,* 61-75.

Schaefer, C.E., Gitlin-Weiner, K., & Sandgrund, A., (2000). *Play diagnosis and assessment* (2nd ed.). New York: Wiley.

Schneck, C.M. (1996). Visual Perception. In J. Case-Smith, A.S. Allen, & P.N. Pratt (Eds.), *Occupational therapy for children* (3rd ed.). St. Louis, MO: Mosby.

Stern, D. N. (1985). *The interpersonal world of the infant.* New York: Basic Books.

Thomas, A., & Chess, S. (1977). *Temperament and development.* New York: Brunner/Mazel.

Tirgal, D., & Bouma, K. (1989). A sensory integration observation guide for children from birth to three years of age. *Sensory Integration Special Interest Newsletter, 12*(2). Rockville, MD: American Occupational Therapy Association.

Wetherby, A. & Prizant, B. (Eds.) (in press). *Communication and language issues in autism and pervasive developmental disabilities: A transactional developmental perspective.* Baltimore: Brookes.

Wilbarger, P. (1995). The sensory diet: Activity programs based on sensory processing theory. *American Occupational Therapy Association Sensory Integration Special Interest Section Quarterly, 18* (2), 1-4.

Wilbarger, P., & Wilbarger, J.L. (1991). *Sensory defensiveness in children aged 2-12: An intervention guide for parents and other caretakers.* Santa Barbara, CA: Avanti Education Programs.

Williams, M.S., & Shellenberger, S. (1996). *How does your engine run?: A leaders guide to the Alert Program for Self-Regulation.* Albuquerque, NM: Therapy Works, Inc.

Williamson, G.G., & Anzalone, M.E. (1997). Sensory integration: A key component of the evaluation and treatment of young children with severe difficulties in relating and communicating. *Zero To Three, 17,* 29-36.

Zeitlin, S., Williamson, G. G., & Szczepanski, M. (1988). *The Early Coping Inventory.* Bensonville, IL: Scholastic Testing Service.

Zeitlin, S., & Williamson, G.G. (1994). *Coping in young children: Early intervention practices to enhance adaptive behavior and resilience.* Baltimore: Brookes.

Zero To Three: National Center for Clinical Infant Programs. (1994). *Diagnostic Classification: 0-3 Diagnostic classification of mental health and developmental disorders of infancy and early childhood.* Arlington, VA: Author.

Zissermann, L. (1992). The effects of deep pressure on self-stimulatory behaviors in a child with autism and other disabilities, *American Journal of Occupational Therapy, 46,* 547-557.

Authors

G. Gordon Williamson, Ph.D., OTR, is the Director of Project BEAM at the John F. Kennedy Medical Center in Edison, New Jersey. This federally funded project provides inservice training in the area of adaptive and social competence to agencies serving families living in urban poverty. He is also an Associate Clinical Professor in the College of Physicians and Surgeons of Columbia University. Dr. Williamson is a member of the Board of Directors of ZERO TO THREE: National Center for Infants, Toddlers and Families and the American Occupational Therapy Foundation. Previously, he chaired the Parental and Child Health Advisory Committee of the New Jersey Department of Health and served as an officer of the Division for Early Childhood/Council for Exceptional Children. Dr. Williamson has lectured extensively throughout the United States, South America and the Middle East. His most recent book is *Coping in Young Children: Early Intervention Practices To Enhance Adaptive Behavior and Resilience.* His research focuses on the study of the coping resources of children and their families.

Marie Anzalone, Sc.D., OTR, FAOTA, is Assistant Professor of Clinical Occupational Therapy at Columbia University. She has extensive experience in pediatric occupational therapy, specializing in sensory integration with the young child, neonatology, and self and mutual regulation during mother-infant play. She has completed both her masters degree in occupational therapy and doctorate in Therapeutic Studies at Boston University's Sargent College of Allied Health Professions. Dr. Anzalone is a Graduate Fellow of ZERO TO THREE: National Center for Infants, Toddlers, and Families, and a Fellow of the

American Occupational Therapy Association. Her current research focuses on mother-child interaction during play and the efficacy of sensory integration intervention with children who have autism.